THE IMMACULATE HEART of MARY
and God's Plan for America

LUIZ SÉRGIO SOLIMEO

---

*In commemoration of the 100th
Anniversary of the Apparitions
of Our Lady of Fatima
1917-2017*

America Needs Fatima
P.O. Box 341, Hanover, PA 17331
(888) 317-5571
ANF@ANF.org • www.ANF.org

To order more copies of this book, please contact:
America Needs Fatima
P.O. Box 341, Hanover, PA 17331
(888) 317-5571
ANF@ANF.org • www.ANF.org

The statue of the Immaculate of Heart of Mary printed on the front cover and pages 28 and 58 is located in the Basilica of Our Lady of Sorrows, operated by the Servite Fathers. The Basilica is located at 3121 W. Jackson Blvd, Chicago, IL 60612. Phone: (773) 638-0159 Web: www.ols-chicago.org

Cover design: MaryDes
Book design: Elizabeth Saracino

ISBN: 978-1-877905-49-0
Library of Congress Control Number: 2016958672

Second Printing
Printed in the United States of America

THE IMMACULATE HEART of MARY
and God's Plan for America

CONTENTS

FOREWORD

Public and Private Devotion to the Immaculate Heart of Mary

The Core of Our Lady's Fatima Requests

BY JOSEPH M. SCHEIDLER

When the soldier saw that the crucified Christ was already dead, he thrust a lance into His side, piercing His Heart. Over time, Christians began to honor this pierced Heart with a special devotion to the Sacred Heart of Jesus, always pictured with the wound, the crown of thorns and a flame of divine mercy flowing from the Heart. This devotion was made popular throughout the Catholic world by Christ's appearance to Saint Margaret Mary Alacoque in 1673, and few churches today lack an image or statue of Christ pointing to His Sacred Heart.

But Mary herself revealed that her Immaculate Heart beats as one with the Heart of her Son and that devotion to her Heart is critical in these times to bring about the conversion of our society. Particular to this devotion was Mary's appearance to three children at Fatima in 1917. This was one of those times that Mary left her eternal home in heaven to break into human time. She appeared to Lúcia, Jacinta and Francisco six times and made it clear that unless devotion to her Immaculate Heart was spread throughout the world there would be dire consequences.

She foretold impending war, famine, the spread of communism and a general secularizing of society. The message of Fatima has been virtually ignored and we have seen the terrible consequences of the First World War, a moral collapse in almost every society, great depressions, the plague of Fascism and Nazism, a Second World War taking sixty million lives, nuclear terror and the spread of communism throughout the world.

In addition to these plagues on society is the emergence of

wayward youth, the breakdown of marriage, transgender tyranny, wars in the east, widespread abortion and a crisis of modernism throughout the world. Even within the Catholic Church, we find a great fall in attendance at Mass, liberation theology and relative morality and clergy who openly espouse positions in opposition to Church teaching.

The only bright spot in this litany of trouble is Mary's promise at Fatima that her Immaculate Heart would triumph in the end. In fact, the devotion to the Immaculate Heart of Mary permeates the message of Fatima.

Though Mary has a purely human heart, Christ chose her to be co-redeemer with Him, that her divine motherhood of the Incarnate Word makes her a spiritual mother of us all. When Jesus gave Mary to Saint John and thus to us on Calvary, He was teaching us that we have a direct route to Him through our Mother, who cares deeply about our welfare and wants to lead us to an eternal home with her Son. She suffered the passion and death of Jesus as no one else ever has.

Her Seven Sorrows are a testimony to her suffering with her Son, from the prophecy of Simeon to the flight into Egypt, the loss of Christ in the temple, following Him on the way of His cross and standing beneath His cross when He died, feeling the lance and laying Him in His tomb. Just as we draw strength from the Sacred Heart of Jesus, we draw strength from Mary's Immaculate Heart. But Mary asks more than devotion. She asks for a consecration to her Immaculate Heart. Mary specifically asked for the consecration of Russia to her Immaculate Heart.

At Fatima, Mary emphasized the praying of the daily Rosary and introduced a new devotion of reparation—receiving Holy Communion, going to confession and meditating on the mysteries of the Rosary on the first Saturday of five consecutive months. In return, she promised special assistance at the hour of death.

In 2017 the world will celebrate the centennial of Mary's six apparitions at Fatima. In the midst of the downward spiral of the secular word, millions of faithful have responded to the message she delivered to the shepherd children. And we are witnessing the fulfillment of her promises.

Solimeo borrows heavily from Saint Louis de Montfort in identifying the authentic signs of devotion to the Immaculate Heart of Mary. It must be interior, flowing from the spirit of deep love for Mary and Jesus. It must be tender, full of the confidence of a child toward his mother. In any crisis the soul will turn to Mary. It must be holy, as sinless as humanly possible. It must be constant. And it must be disinterested, that is, not self-seeking, but pursued simply because she is worthy of such love and devotion.

The Immaculate Heart of Mary and God's Plan for America is a book for our times. If there ever was a need for an insightful explanation of this special form of prayer and dedication it is now. Mary herself has called for it. By this means, she promises a solution to the terrible plights of our society today.

There is a maxim that applies itself most directly to this book, "Never say 'no' to your mother."

INTRODUCTION

Procession in Fatima, Portugal (May 13, 2016).

The Importance of the Fatima Centennial

O n July 13, 1917, in the small town of Fatima, Portugal, Our Lady told the three shepherd children, Lúcia, Francisco, and Jacinta, that in October she would perform a miracle so that all might believe in the apparitions. Word of the promised miracle spread, and some 70,000 pilgrims from all walks of life, and from all parts of the country, made their way to that remote mountainous region—some in vehicles, but most on foot, and in the rain—to see what would happen.

As Mary promised, one hundred years ago, the most impressive event in Church history since the days of the Apostles took place on October 13th. Thousands of people, soaked by rain that had fallen unceasingly for days, unexpectedly saw the clouds open up, and the sun shine brightly. Then, suddenly, they witnessed an apocalyptic spectacle: the sun began to zigzag—"dance," one newspaper of the time called it—and fall towards the earth. The crowd sank to their knees, confessing their sins aloud, and asking for God's forgiveness. They thought the world was coming to an end.

Thus, a crowd of thousands became the witnesses of the miracle of the sun!

Recalling Biblical Times

This dramatic event, almost Biblical in nature, calls to mind Joshua's "miracle of the sun," from the Old Testament.[1] Even unbelievers were amazed. Avelino de Almeida, an agnostic journalist writing for Lisbon's anticlerical daily newspaper, *O Século*, described the event in the October 15 (1917) edition:

> Many pilgrims say the miraculous manifestation, the visible

---

[1] Cf. Joshua 10:13.

sign announced, is about to happen.... And then one witnesses a spectacle unique and unbelievable for someone not there to see it. From the top of the road...one sees the huge crowd turn toward the sun, now freed from the clouds, at its zenith. The sun resembles a plate of opaque silver and one can look at it without any strain. It does not burn or blind. One would say an eclipse is taking place. Then a huge roar comes from the crowd and those closer to the place cry out:

"Miracle, miracle! Marvel, marvel!"

As the peasants typically put it, the sun "danced," shook and made abrupt movements outside all cosmic laws as those people filled with awe, with an attitude that recalls biblical times, heads uncovered, looked up into the blue with their fascinated eyes.... It is close to three o'clock p.m.[2]

Message of Punishment and Hope

Why did Our Lady perform this stupendous miracle?

She did it to confirm her decisive message for our times, warning us of the consequences of sin: Hell in the afterlife for those who die without repenting, and, in this life, the punishment of nations.

She showed Hell to the little children, saying it is "where the souls of poor sinners go."[3] She also spoke about a new world war and the expansion of communism if men did not amend their ways.

As a mother, she presented the means to avoid this individual and collective punishment: devotion to her Immaculate Heart.

In opposition to sin's personal and collective dimensions, she wanted us to practice this devotion both privately and publicly. From each of us individually, she asked that we demonstrate our devotion to her Immaculate Heart through the recitation of the Holy Rosary, the practice of the Five First Saturdays and

---

[2] Luiz Sérgio Solimeo, *Fatima: A Message More Urgent than Ever* (Spring Grove, Penn.: The American Society for the Defense of Tradition, Family and Property—TFP, 2008), 83-4.

[3] Ibid., 49.

the Communion of Reparation. From all of us gathered to-gether in society, she asked for this devotion to take on a public scope, especially with the Consecration of Russia by the Holy Father in union with all the world's bishops.

If her requests were not heeded, she said a punishment would start "in the reign of Pius XI."[4] The world did not listen, so World War II and the expansion of communism socially, po-litically, economically, and culturally ensued. Today, cultural communism dominates the world.

This is the message Our Blessed Mother gave to three shep-herd children in Fatima, in 1917, one hundred years ago.

Fatima: the Dawn of a New Era
As we commemorate the centennial of these apparitions, let us remember that commemorating a historical fact is not merely recalling it to mind as one would a history lesson. It is the fes-tive remembrance and praise of something deemed worthy of admiration and emulation, and even devotion.

The apparitions of Our Lady at Fatima were one of the most extraordinary interventions of God in history, both because the message was brought by the Mother of God and because she confirmed it with a great miracle. Plinio Corrêa de Oliveira, a great devotee and apostle of the devotion to Our Lady of Fa-tima, affirms:

> Fatima is a new milestone in the history of the Church. It is...
> the true dawn of a New Era whose early light did not rise from bat-
> tlefields or from the pages of so many writers, but when Our Lady
> descended to earth, communicated to the three children the harsh
> lessons on the twilight of our days, and said hopeful words about
> the happy days that Divine Mercy has in store for mankind, when
> it finally repents.[5]

---

[4] Ibid.

[5] Plinio Corrêa de Oliveira, "Books v. Cannons," *Legionário*, Apr. 8, 1945, accessed Mar. 14, 2016, http://www.pliniocorreadeoliveira.info/LEG%2045-04-08_Livrosversuscanhoes.htm. (Our translation.)

Using the Centennial to Better Understand Fatima

During the past one hundred years, devotion to Our Lady of Fatima has spread throughout the world and her message has become universally known. Numerous books describe and analyze the apparitions, and many organizations promote devotion to Our Lady of Fatima and organize pilgrimages to her shrine in Portugal.

"*De Fatima nunquam satis*" [there is never enough said about Fatima] as Prof. Corrêa de Oliveira states in the article quoted above. The humble goal of this book is to use the centennial, and its special graces, to broaden our understanding of both the message and the events connected to it.

Devotion to the Immaculate Heart of Mary is the central core of the Fatima message. Our Lady's request for Russia's consecration to her Immaculate Heart is particularly prominent in this message. For these reasons, we will be taking a closer look at two points in particular:

1. We will analyze devotion to the Immaculate Heart and what it means, in the context of that devotion, to consecrate oneself or one's country to her Heart.

2. We will probe the meaning of Our Lady's promise of Russia's conversion. We will describe the "errors of Russia" and their relation to the crisis of the modern world, and, more profoundly, to the centuries-long and gradual process of the destruction of Christian civilization which, starting with Protestantism, culminated in communism.

America Needs Fatima promoted an online protest and a public Act of Reparation to God for the opening of the "Greater Church of Lucifer" in Spring, Texas (October, 2015).

CHAPTER 1
Rejection of the Fatima Message and Deserved Punishments

Many fervent Catholics around the world took Our Lady's Fatima message seriously. Unfortunately, however, the majority of people showed indifference, if not open contempt, for the warnings of the Mother of God. In their daily lives, they ignored Our Lady's call to prayer, penance and sacrifice.

A hundred years have passed since the apparitions of Our Lady at Fatima and the world still rejects her twofold request for conversion and for an increase in devotion to the Immaculate Heart of Mary.

"The present moment is the most tragic the Church has seen since the Catacombs," Plinio Corrêa de Oliveira observed. "This portentous scenario is dominated by Our Lady's appearance to the little shepherds. Everything else that happens in the world is in function of her: *Everything is unleashed because Our Lady was not heeded and her request was not obeyed.*"[6]

Consequences of Rejection

What were the consequences of rejecting Our Lady's message?

In Fatima, Our Lady clearly stated that wars are a punishment for the sins of nations. But during these hundred years, the moral decadence of peoples has only increased, and so the world has been punished with wars and other disasters.

We are not saying that many good and even excellent things did not occur during the past hundred years, both in the Church and in society. Good things did happen. The generosity of the American people who sacrificed their lives and shed their blood in wars against Nazism and communism is a perfect example.

Nonetheless, we must always remember that the chastisements God sends us on this earth have two aspects: one is to

---

[6] Plinio Corrêa de Oliveira, Lecture, Nov. 25, 1974 (Archives of the Plinio Corrêa de Oliveira Commission). (Our emphasis.)

make reparation for offenses committed against Him and the other is "medicinal." In their healing role, God's chastisements seek the conversion of sinners and the sanctification of the righteous. The purpose of these sufferings is to teach us detachment from sin and to instill the practice of virtue. This is how God acted in the Old Testament with the Chosen People when they ignored His commandments.

Let us consider some of the calamities—punishments from God—that have occurred since 1917 because of the world's refusal to heed the Blessed Mother's appeal. This will help us grasp better the seriousness of the Fatima message.[7]

List of Tragedies Since 1917
Our Lady's last apparition at Fatima was on October 13, 1917. Within a month, the Bolshevik Communists seized power in Russia.[8] From then until now, the satanic doctrine of communism has spread across the globe.

World War I (1914-1918) resulted in the death of approximately 18 million people and it destroyed Europe's traditional order.

As terrible as that war was, the punishment proved insufficient to bring the world to conversion. Soon after the cannons stopped thundering, a moral calamity swept through the world. Women's fashions abandoned modesty and delicacy, becoming sensual and extravagant. Relations between the sexes lost much of their courteous ceremony and became egalitarian and vulgar. The avid thirst for frenzied pleasures, expressed in dances like the Charleston, turned the 1920s into "the Roaring Twenties" in America, and "*les années folles*" (the crazy years) in France.

---

[7] As the complete list of tragedies would be excessive in length, here we mention only wars and social upheavals that we consider more directly linked to the Fatima message.

[8] By our Gregorian calendar, the Bolshevik Revolution took place on November 7, 1917; but according to the Julian calendar then used in Russia, it was still October 25th. Hence, it was called the "October Revolution."

The world economy collapsed with the Great Depression. At the same time, social unrest became widespread, almost paralyzing Germany, France, Italy and other countries.

Amid the disorder, the false solutions of Fascism and Nazism emerged on the Old Continent. Both promised order, but not true order that arises from a Christian organic society, but a totalitarian order imposed by an authoritarian state.[9]

The 1930s were a long preparation for World War II, which caused over 60 million deaths. The atomic bombs dropped on Hiroshima and Nagasaki opened a new era: nuclear terror.

Because of the February 1945 Yalta agreement between the governments of Britain, the United States, and Russia, all of Eastern Europe fell under Soviet domination. It was a betrayal of the hopes of millions who had fought and died. In 1949, China, too, was betrayed and fell to communism. From there, it spread throughout Southeast Asia. Thus, Our Lady's prophecy at Fatima that the "errors of Russia" would spread around the world was being fulfilled.

After World War II, just as in the 1920s, instead of heeding Our Lady's call to conversion, society again plunged into the pursuit of pleasure and material wealth. Unfortunately, America's wealth, prestige, and influence were not matched by proportional spiritual progress.

In the 1950s, the "wayward youth" phenomenon appeared. Intoxicated with the irrational excitement of rock n' roll, many youngsters revolted against a society that gave them everything—everything, that is, except the things that give life purpose and meaning. Although these liberals were a minority among American youth, films like *Rebel Without a Cause* (1955) and *Rock Around the Clock* (1956) spread that way of being all over the world.

---

[9] Cf. John Horvat II, *Return to Order: From a Frenzied Economy to an Organic Christian Society—Where We've Been, How We Got Here, and Where We Need to Go* (York, Penn.: York Press, 2013).

Rebel Without a Cause prepared the student revolt, sexual revolution, and the "counterculture" of the 1960s, blending sexual freedom and political anarchism. That mix gave rise to the hippie, feminist, and homosexual movements. The groundwork was laid for the irrationality of today's same-sex "marriage" and transgender tyranny.

Between 1950 and 1953, the Korean War claimed more than 600,000 victims. Roughly at the same time (1946-1954), the French waged war in Indochina against communist troops armed and supported by Red China. More than 400,000 soldiers and civilians died during the conflict.

Still in the 1950s, communist guerrilla warfare began in Latin America. In 1959, under the dictatorship of brothers Fidel and Raul Castro, Cuba became the first communist country in the Western Hemisphere. The enslavement of the Cuban people continues to this day. An estimated 100,000 people have perished trying to escape the Island Prison by sea.

In 1965, the American phase of the Vietnam War began—a "no-win war" as the Korean War had been before it. It ended with the withdrawal of U.S. troops and the fall of Saigon in 1975. The war served as a pretext for the left to promote violent protests and riots in the United States. The death toll of the Vietnam War, including soldiers and non-combatants, was 1,313,000.

According to estimates published by *The Black Book of Communism: Crimes, Terror, Repression*,[10] those killed by communism throughout the world, from 1917 until today, total 94 million.

Throughout most of the 20th century, a Modernist crisis festered just beneath the surface of the Catholic Church. After the Second Vatican Council (1962-1965), this Modernist crisis

---

[10] Stéphane Courtois et al, *The Black Book of Communism: Crimes, Terror, Repression*, ed. Mark Kramer (Cambridge, Mass.: Harvard University Press, 1999).

erupted into plain view. In the years immediately following the Council, tens of thousands of priests, and men and women religious, left the ministry throughout the world. The number of priestly and religious vocations dropped dramatically. In the United States, the number of priests dropped from 58,632 in 1965 to 38,275 in 2010; the number of women religious, from about 200,000 in 1965 to 56,000 in 2010; their average age is now 74. Attendance at Sunday Mass fell from 55% in 1965 to a mere 24% in 2010.[11]

Latin America suffered the rise of "liberation theology,"[12] a strongly Marxist-oriented movement that, in addition to social strife, triggered a massive exodus of Catholics to other religions. In Brazil, the world's largest Catholic country, the Catholic population fell from 93.1% in 1960 to 64.6% in 2010.

In 1968, when the Encyclical *Humanae Vitae* was published condemning contraception (birth control through mechanical devices, chemical drugs or surgery), it encountered stiff resistance worldwide from liberal bishops and clergy, and the (not-so) faithful that listened to them.

Today, the Church is rife with public discord among cardinals and bishops over fundamental teachings of the Catholic Faith: for example, the giving of Holy Communion to people living objectively in the state of adultery, i.e. public mortal sin. We see the same discord regarding homosexual sin and same-sex "marriage."[13]

A new type of war afflicts the world. Some call it "asymmetric

---

[11] Cf. Center for Applied Research in the Apostolate, Frequently Requested Church Statistics, accessed Mar. 14, 2016, http://cara.georgetown.edu/frequently-requested-church-statistics/; Michael Wineripdec, "The Vanishing of the Nuns," New York Times, Dec. 2, 2012, accessed Mar. 14, 2016, http://www.nytimes.com/2012/12/02/booming/the-vanishing-of-the-nuns.html.

[12] Cf. Gustavo Antonio Solimeo and Luiz Sérgio Solimeo, *Grassroots Church Communities (GRCGs): Perestroika in Latin America?* (Carmel, N.Y.: Western Hemisphere Cultural Society, Inc., 1991) Chapter II — "Liberation Theology: The Doctrine of the Grassroots."

[13] Cf. Nicole Winfield and Ines San Martin, "Cardinals Publicly Battling over Divorce," accessed Mar. 14, 2016, http://www.cruxnow.com/church/2014/09/18/walter-kasper-cardinals-debate-marriage-ahead-of-crucial-meeting/.

warfare." Others say that we are already in World War III. Today's wars involve not just nation-states, as the First and Second Gulf Wars did), but also new (and especially Islamist) terrorist organizations that fight against nations. As we all know, Al Qaeda and ISIS (Islamic State) are active in the Middle East and Africa, as well as in Europe and the United States.

Europe is being "softly" invaded by migrants and refugees from predominantly Muslim countries. Simultaneously, terrorist attacks, including "rape jihad" (abuse of Western Christian women in the name of Islam), have increased in the United Kingdom, France, Germany, Belgium, Denmark, Sweden, the Netherlands, and other countries.

Today, the sexual revolution of the sixties is now manifesting itself in ever-more shocking ways such as can be seen in the promotion of the transgender and identity issues that destroy the distinctions between the sexes and introduce new "genders" and behaviors that are contrary to Christian morality.

These events acquire new meaning when pondered in the light of Fatima. It appears that a contraction of divine grace has occurred as a result of the refusal to heed the Mother of God's call to conversion.

There is, however, no reason to despair. The same message of Fatima promises the triumph of the Immaculate Heart of Mary. To hasten that triumph we must pray, sacrifice, and, above all, spread devotion to the maternal Heart.

CHAPTER 2
The Immaculate Heart of Mary:
Core of the Fatima Message

Devotion to the Immaculate Heart of Mary permeates the whole story and message of Fatima. One may well say that it is the very core of the message, as well as the solution presented for the problems of today's world.

Jesus Wants Devotion to the Immaculate Heart

In 1916, the angel[14] who came to prepare the three shepherd children for the apparitions of the Blessed Virgin said to them, "The Hearts of Jesus and Mary are attentive to the voice of your supplications."[15]

In another apparition, the angel repeated the message: "Pray! Pray a great deal! The Most Sacred Hearts of Jesus and Mary have merciful designs for you."[16]

The Mother of God herself, in the second apparition, told Lúcia:

> Jesus wishes to make use of you to make me known and loved. He wishes to establish in the world devotion to my Immaculate Heart. To those who embrace it, I promise salvation. And these souls will be beloved by God like flowers placed by me to adorn His throne.[17]

Upon learning that she was going to be alone on earth after the death of her cousins, Lúcia was distressed. The Blessed Virgin consoled her, saying: "I will never forsake you. My Immaculate Heart will be your refuge and the road that will lead you to God."[18]

These two statements—that Jesus wants to establish devotion to the Immaculate Heart of Mary in the world, and that

---

[14] During the course of 1916, an angel appeared three times to the three children to prepare them for the heavenly events of the following year. Imitating this "Angel of Peace" in prayer and encouraged by him to offer sacrifices, they were then fortified by this "Angel of Portugal" with the Bread of Angels in Holy Communion.

[15] Solimeo, *Fatima*, 25.

[16] Ibid., 26.

[17] Ibid., 41.

[18] Ibid.

her Immaculate Heart is the refuge of suffering souls and the path that leads to heaven—summarize Fatima spirituality.

Devotion of Reparation

Due reparation for the continuous offenses perpetrated against the Immaculate Heart today is the essence of this devotion.

Thus, soon after Our Lady's words quoted above, the seers described what they saw, inside a bright light: "In front of the palm of Our Lady's right hand was a heart surrounded with thorns which seemed to be piercing it. We understood that it was the Immaculate Heart of Mary, outraged by the sins of humanity, which wanted reparation."[19]

Our Lady gave her message on July 13th, during the third and most important apparition. She insisted on the reparative aspect of the devotion: "Sacrifice yourselves for sinners and say many times, especially when you make some sacrifice, 'O Jesus, it is for Thy love, for the conversion of sinners and in reparation for the sins committed against the Immaculate Heart of Mary.'"[20]

Remedy to Save Souls and the World

After showing Hell to the little shepherds, she continued:

> You have seen Hell, where the souls of poor sinners go. To save them, God wishes to establish devotion to my Immaculate Heart in the world. If they do what I will tell you, many souls will be saved, and there will be peace. The war is going to end. But if they do not stop offending God, another even worse war will begin in the reign of Pius XI. When you see a night illuminated by an unknown light, know that it is the great sign that God gives you that He is going to punish the world for its crimes by means of war, hunger, and persecutions against the Church and the Holy Father.
>
> To prevent it [the war] I will come to ask the consecration of

---

[19] Ibid.

[20] Ibid., 47-8.

Russia to my Immaculate Heart and the Communion of Reparation on the First Saturdays. If they listen to my requests, Russia will
be converted and there will be peace. If not, she will scatter her errors throughout the world, provoking wars and persecutions of the
Church. The good will be martyred, the Holy Father will have much
to suffer and various nations will be annihilated. In the end, my
Immaculate Heart will triumph. The Holy Father will consecrate
Russia to me and she will be converted and a certain period of
peace will be granted to the world. In Portugal the dogma of the
Faith will always be preserved. . . .[21]

A Penitential Devotion

After the apparitions, one day when Lúcia was visiting Jacinta, who
was already approaching her premature death, she said to Lúcia:

Our Lady came to see us and said she will come to take Francisco to heaven very soon. And she asked me if I still wanted to
convert more sinners. I told her yes. She said I would be going to a
hospital where I would have much to suffer; that I should suffer for
the conversion of sinners, in reparation for the sins against the Immaculate Heart of Mary, and for the love of Jesus.[22]

In 1921, sometime after the death of her cousins, Lúcia
moved to the Vilar convent in Porto, an institution of the Sisters
of Saint Dorothy, where she continued her studies. In 1925, she
joined that religious congregation and became a postulant in
Pontevedra, Spain. It was then that she was tasked, in a vision,
with asking for the reparative devotion of the First Saturdays.

Though it may sound odd to the modern reader, her narra-
tion is in the third person for humility's sake. She says:

On December 10, 1925, the most Holy Virgin appeared to [Sister
Lúcia] and beside her, suspended on a luminous cloud, was a Boy.
The most Holy Virgin rested her hand on Sister Lúcia's shoulder and
at the same time showed her a heart surrounded with thorns in her
other hand.

---

[21] Ibid., 49-50.

[22] Ibid., 94.

At the same time, the Boy said, "Have pity on the Heart of your Most Holy Mother that is covered with thorns with which ungrateful men pierce it at every moment with no one to make an act of reparation to pull them out."

Then, the Virgin said, "See, my daughter, my Heart surrounded with the thorns with which ungrateful men pierce me at every moment by their blasphemies and ingratitude. You, at least, try to console me and say that all those who for five months, on the first Saturday, go to Confession, receive Communion, say five decades of the Rosary and keep me company for fifteen minutes meditating on the mysteries of the Rosary, with the purpose of making reparation to me, I promise to assist them at the hour of death with all the graces necessary for the salvation of their souls."[23]

The Five Offenses Committed
Against the Immaculate Heart

In a letter of June 12, 1930, to her confessor, answering his questions on the First Saturdays' devotion, in particular, "Why does it have to be five Saturdays, and not nine or seven in honor of the sorrows of Our Lady?" Sister Lúcia explained:

While staying in the chapel with Our Lord part of the night between the twenty-ninth to the thirtieth of the month of May, 1930, and speaking to Our Lord, I suddenly felt more intimately possessed by the Divine Presence, and if I am not mistaken, the following was revealed to me, "My daughter, the reason is simple. There are five kinds of offenses and blasphemies perpetrated against the Immaculate Heart of Mary: blasphemies against her Immaculate Conception; against her virginity; against her divine maternity, at the same time refusing to accept her as the Mother of men; those who try publicly to instill indifference, contempt and even hatred toward this Immaculate Mother in the hearts of children; and those who insult her directly in her sacred images."[24]

---

[23] Ibid., 103-4.

[24] Ibid., 105.

CHAPTER 3
Symbolism of the Heart

Symbolic Language

Man expresses his ideas not only through concepts and words, but also through symbols.

Symbols are sensible signs that evoke or represent a higher and more abstract reality. For example, the national flag represents the homeland; the lily evokes purity; the scepter and crown represent royal power.

Of all symbols, the human heart is perhaps the most common and universal.

Closely linked to emotions that alter one's heartbeat, the heart symbolizes one's preference, and especially one's love. A mother's heart, for example, is a symbol of selfless love, full of affection and unconditionally capable of the greatest sacrifices. On the other hand, the epithet of Richard I of England (1157-1199), "the Lion-Hearted," expresses his fearlessness, courage, indomitable prowess, and indefatigable combativeness.

Heart Symbolism in Sacred Scripture

Father Maximo Peinador, CMF, explains the symbolic use of the "heart" in Scripture:

> [The heart] is used very often to indicate man's interior as opposed to his exterior, that is, his soul, his conscience...more frequently, to express emotions or feelings of the soul...and thus, we attribute to the heart blindness of mind and hardness of soul, desire, delight, joy, mercy, pain, etc.... The Bible speaks of the wise, prudent heart, of thoughts of the heart.[25]

---

[25] Maximo Peinador, CMF, *Teologia Biblica Cordimariana* (Madrid: Editorial Coculsa, 1959), 47. (Our translation.) See also Gen. 6:5, Psalms 32:11, Prov. 6:18, 15:14, 18:15; Sirach 3:32, Luke 2:35; Eph. 1:18: "the eyes of your heart."

French exegete Fr. Xavier Léon-Dufour makes a similar commentary:

> In the Bible's concrete and global anthropology, man's heart is the very source of his conscious, intelligent and free personality, the place of his decisive choices, the place of unwritten Law (Rom. 2:15) and of the mysterious action of God. In the Old and New Testaments, the heart is the place where man meets God, an encounter that becomes permanent, effective in the human heart of the Son of God.[26]

Biblical Texts

Several examples of the various symbolic meanings of the word *heart* are found in both the Old and New Testaments:

1) The Heart as Center of Human Decision Making

"[O]ut of the *abundance of the heart* the mouth speaks" (Matt. 12:34).

"But the things which proceed out of the mouth, *come forth from the heart*, and those things defile a man. For from the heart come forth evil thoughts, murders, adulteries, fornications, thefts, false testimonies, blasphemies" (Matt. 15:18-19).

"A *perverse heart* is abominable to the Lord: and his will is in them that walk sincerely" (Prov. 11:20).

"He that is of a *perverse heart*, shall not find good: and he that perverted his tongue, shall fall into evil" (Prov. 17:20).

"*The heart is perverse* above all things, *and unsearchable*, who can know it? *I am the Lord who search the heart* and prove the reins: who give to every one according to his way, and according to the fruit of his devices" (Jer. 17:9-10).

2) Inner Center of Man's Thoughts

"And *these words* which I command thee this day, shall be in *thy heart*" (Deut. 6:6).

---

[26] Xavier Léon-Dufour, *Vocabulário de Teologia Bíblica* (Petrópolis: Vozes, 1992), 175. (Our translation.)

"Let not mercy and truth leave thee, put them about thy neck, and *write* them in the tablet of *thy heart*" (Prov. 3:3). "A good man out of the good *treasure of his heart* bringeth forth that which is good: and an evil man out of the evil treasure bringeth forth that which is evil" (Luke 6:45).

3) Where Conversion Takes Place
"Create a *clean heart* in me, O God: and renew a right spirit within my bowels" (Ps. 50:12).
"Let my heart be undefiled in thy justifications, that I may not be confounded" (Ps. 118:80).
"And *rend your hearts*, and *not your garments*, and turn to the Lord your God" (Joel 2:13).

4) In Connection with Chastity and Upright Intentions
"Who shall ascend into the mountain of the Lord: or who shall stand in his Holy place? The innocent in hands, and *clean of heart*, who hath not taken his soul in vain, nor sworn deceitfully to his neighbor" (Ps. 23:3-4).
"Blessed are the *clean of heart*: for they shall see God" (Matt. 5:8).
"My son, *give me thy heart*: and let thy eyes keep my ways" (Prov. 23:26).

5) Seat of Faith and Love
"Let us draw near with a *true heart* in fullness of faith" (Heb. 10:22).
"That *Christ* may *dwell* by faith *in your hearts*" (Eph. 3:17).
"For if thou confess with thy mouth the Lord Jesus, and *believe in thy heart* that God hath raised him up from the dead, thou shalt be saved. For, *with the heart*, we believe unto justice; but, with the mouth, confession is made unto salvation" (Rom. 10:9-10).

6) Where the Natural Law Is Inscribed

"For if *our heart reprehend* us, God is *greater than our heart,* and knows all things" (1 John 3:20).

"For when the Gentiles, who have not the law [of Moses], do by nature those things that are of the law; these having not the law are a law to themselves: Who show the work of *the law written in their hearts,* their conscience bearing witness to them, and their thoughts between themselves accusing, or also defending one another" (Rom. 2:14-15).

7) Fountain of Life

"With all watchfulness keep thy *heart,* because *life issued out from it*" (Prov. 4:23).

"[A]nd I will take away the *stony heart* out of your flesh, and will give you *a heart of flesh*" (Ezekiel 36:26).

CHAPTER 4
The Sacred Heart of Jesus

We cannot speak of the Immaculate Heart of Mary without mentioning the Sacred Heart of Jesus, the model and source from which the devotion to the Heart of Mary comes.

Devotion to the Sacred Heart is more than just the worship of this noble part of our adorable Savior's body. In the Sacred Heart, we adore the very Person of the Incarnate Word with all His Divine and human attributes. The Sacred Heart is the symbol of the redeeming love of Our Lord Jesus Christ for men and represents the most ardent affections of the God-Man in His Incarnation, Passion, Death, and Resurrection.

In expounding on this holy devotion, there is nothing better than the Encyclical *Haurietis Aquas*, in which Pope Pius XII (1939-1958) summarized it with unction and solid theological foundation.[27]

The Popes Speak on the Importance of Devotion to the Sacred Heart

Fighting the naturalist mentality opposed to this devotion, the Pope dispels the objections that it is sentimental and only suitable for older women.[28] On the contrary, he says, devotion to the Sacred Heart of Jesus is not unmanly; the consideration of Our Lord's merciful love, represented by His heart, is the quintessence of devotion to the Savior.[29] And, the Pope states:

> If we consider its special nature it is beyond question that this devotion [to the Sacred Heart] is an act of religion of high order; it

---

[27] Pius XII, Encyclical *Haurietis Aquas* (On Devotion to the Sacred Heart), May 15, 1956, accessed May 24, 2016, http://www.vatican.va/holy_father/pius_xii/encyclicals/documents/hf_p-xii_enc_15051956_haurietis-aquas_en.html.

[28] Cf. Ibid., no. 12.

[29] Cf. Ibid., no. 14.

demands of us a complete and unreserved determination to devote and consecrate ourselves to the love of the divine Redeemer, Whose wounded Heart is its living token and symbol.[30]

For this reason, he continues,

> [T]he Church has always valued, and still does, the devotion to the Most Sacred Heart of Jesus so highly that she provides for the spread of it among Christian peoples everywhere and by every means. At the same time she uses every effort to protect it against the charges of so-called "naturalism" and "sentimentalism."[31]

In the words of Pope Leo XIII (1878-1903), "This world-wide and solemn testimony of allegiance and piety is especially appropriate."[32] And, as Pope Pius XI (1922-1939) stated, this devotion is "the sum of all religion."[33]

This devotion, continues Pius XII, "more easily leads our minds to know Christ the Lord intimately and more effectively turns our hearts to love Him more ardently and to imitate Him more perfectly."[34]

For all these reasons, Pope Pius XII deems it, "a powerful remedy for the healing of those very evils which today also, and beyond question in a wider and more serious way, bring distress and disquiet to individuals and to the whole human race."[35]

Theological Basis of Devotion to the Sacred Heart

The Encyclical *Haurietis Aquas* gives the theological reasons for devotion to the Sacred Heart. Due to the limited scope of this

---

[30] Ibid., no. 6.

[31] Ibid., no. 8.

[32] Leo XIII, Encyclical *Annum Sacrum*, May 25, 1899, no. 3, accessed May 20, 2016, http://w2.vatican.va/content/leo-xiii/en/encyclicals/documents/hf_l-xiii_enc_25051899_annum-sacrum.html.

[33] Pius XI, Encyclical *Miserentissimus Redemptor*, May 8, 1928, no. 3, accessed May 20, 2016, http://w2.vatican.va/content/pius-xi/en/encyclicals/documents/hf_p-xi_enc_19280508_miserentissimus-redemptor.html.

[34] Pius XII, Enc. *Haurietis Aquas,* no. 15.

[35] Ibid., no. 14.

book, we present only a summary of the rich argumentation developed by Pius XII. However, we highly recommend the full text of the encyclical for its beauty and soothing remedy.[36]

Our Lord's Heart, the Pontiff teaches, "the noblest part of human nature, is hypostatically united to the Person of the Divine Word." For this reason, "there must be paid to it that worship of adoration with which the Church honors the Person of the Incarnate Son of God Himself."[37]

Furthermore, the Sacred Heart, "more than all the other members of His body, is the natural sign and symbol of His boundless love for the human race." This heart symbolizes and expresses "the infinite love of Jesus Christ which moves us to love in return."[38]

Although Sacred Scripture does not directly mention the worship and veneration of the Sacred Heart, it does express "the divine love for us which is the principal object of this devotion." On the other hand, it also presents God's love for us with images that recall sensible human love.

> Since these images were presented in the Sacred Writings foretelling the coming of the Son of God made man, they can be considered as a token of the noblest symbol and witness of that divine love, that is, of the most Sacred and Adorable Heart of the Divine Redeemer.[39]

The mystery of our redemption is, above all, a mystery of love: "that is, of the perfect love of Christ for His heavenly Father to Whom the sacrifice of the Cross, offered in a spirit of love and obedience, presents the most abundant and infinite satisfaction due for the sins of the human race."[40]

God's love is purely spiritual, for "God is a spirit." (John 4:24).

---

[36] Cf. Ibid., nos. 21-41.

[37] Ibid., no. 21.

[38] Ibid., no. 22.

[39] Ibid., no. 23.

[40] Ibid., no. 35.

In Christ Our Lord, this love is also sensible because "the Word of God did not assume a feigned and unsubstantial body" but "He united to His divine Person a truly human nature, individual, whole and perfect, which was conceived in the most pure womb of the Virgin Mary by the power of the Holy Ghost."[41] Possessing a truly perfect human nature, Jesus had

> [A]ll the affections proper to the same, among which love surpassed all the rest, it is likewise beyond doubt that He was endowed with a physical heart like ours; for without this noblest part of the body the ordinary emotions of human life are impossible. Therefore the Heart of Jesus Christ, hypostatically united to the divine Person of the Word, certainly beat with love and with the other emotions, but these, joined to a human will full of divine charity and to the infinite love itself which the Son shares with the Father and the Holy Spirit, were in such complete unity and agreement that never among these three loves was there any contradiction or disharmony.[42]

---

[41] Ibid., no. 39.
[42] Ibid., no. 41.

CHAPTER 5
The Immaculate Heart of Mary

Just as devotion to the Sacred Heart of Jesus is essential, for it highlights the redeeming love of the Incarnate Word, so also is devotion to the Immaculate Heart of Mary, since it emphasizes the co-redeeming love of the Mother of God. In the words of Fr. Joaquin Maria Alonso, CMF,

> All devotions [to Mary] are partial manifestations of a single substratum which is Mary's personal love to God and men; devotion to the Heart of Mary directly posits that personal, underpinning love. When this devotion is earnest and lived intensely, it informs all [other devotions], penetrating them with its strong and rich sap.[43]

A Tender Heart, Full of Compassion

Unlike the Heart of Jesus, the Heart of Mary does not participate in the hypostatic union and is, therefore, a purely human heart. It is the heart of the most perfect of creatures who took the love of God to the highest point possible and was closely united to the Heart of Jesus in a maternal and filial intimacy. This intimacy began with the Incarnation of the Word in her most pure womb, culminated with her final offering on Calvary—where She offered her Son for our salvation—and continues now in Heaven.

By the Heart of Mary, as Fr. José Maria Canal, CMF, explains, "we understand her intimacy, maternal feelings, mercy and tenderness toward sinners."[44] For Pope Pius XII it is "a symbol of all interior life, whose moral perfection, merits and virtues are beyond all human understanding!"[45]

Pius XII also emphasizes this maternal Heart's compassion:

---

[43] Joaquin Maria Alonso, CMF, "La Consagración al Corazón de Maria—Una Síntesis Teológica," in José Maria Canal, CMF, *La Consagración al Corazón de María* (Madrid: Editorial Coculsa, 1960), 45. (Our translation.)

[44] José Maria Canal, CMF, *La Consagración a la Virgen y a su Corazón*, I, 250. (Our translation.)

[45] Pius XII, Radio Message to the National Marian Congress in Spain, Oct. 12, 1954, in *Discorsi e Radiomessasaggi*, t. XVI, 197. (Our translation.)

"The Most Pure Heart of the Virgin [is the] seat of that love, compassion and all most lofty affections that participated so much in our redemption, especially when She *stabat iuxta Crucem,* stood vigilantly next to the Cross (cf. John 19:25)."[46]

Heart of the Mother of God and Co-Redemptrix

The theological basis for devotion to the Heart of Mary is three-fold: her collaboration in our redemption, by divine will; her divine Motherhood of the Incarnate Word; and her spiritual motherhood of all men.

There is no better presentation of the doctrinal foundations of this devotion than the aforementioned Encyclical *Haurietis Aquas* of Pius XII, as outlined below.

Co-Redeemer of Mankind by Divine Will

"[B]y God's Will, in carrying out the work of human Redemption the Blessed Virgin Mary was inseparably linked with Christ in such a manner that *our salvation sprang from the love and the sufferings of Jesus Christ to which the love and sorrows of His Mother were intimately united.*"

Mary Most Holy Consented to the Incarnation of the Word

"The adorable Heart of Jesus Christ began to beat with a love at once human and divine after the Virgin Mary generously pronounced Her 'Fiat.'"

Through Her Divine Maternity, She Became the Spiritual Mother of Men

"She who gave birth to our Savior according to the flesh and *was associated with Him in recalling the children of Eve to the life of divine grace has deservedly been hailed as the spiritual Mother of the whole human race.* And so Saint

---

[46] Ibid.

Augustine writes of her: 'Clearly She is Mother of the members of the Savior (which is what we are), because She labored with Him in love that the faithful who are members of the Head might be born in the Church.' (De *sancta virginitate*, VI: P.L. XL, 39974)."

Therefore, Devotion to the Sacred Heart of Jesus and the Heart of Mary Must Go Together
"In order that favors in greater abundance may flow on all Christians, nay, on the whole human race, from the *devotion to the most Sacred Heart of Jesus*, let the faithful see to it that to this *devotion the Immaculate Heart of the Mother of God is closely joined*.... It is, then, entirely fitting that the *Christian people—who received the divine life from Christ through Mary—after they have paid their debt of honor to the Sacred Heart of Jesus should also offer to the most loving Heart of their heavenly Mother* the corresponding acts of piety, affection, gratitude and expiation. Entirely in keeping with this most sweet and wise disposition of divine Providence is the memorable act of consecration by which We Ourselves solemnly dedicated Holy Church and the whole world to the spotless Heart of the Blessed Virgin Mary."[47]

It is most befitting, therefore, for us to have an ardent devotion to the Immaculate Heart of Mary in union with our devotion to the Most Sacred Heart of Jesus.

---

[47] Pius XII, Enc. *Haurietis Aquas*, nos. 63, 72, 124.

Immaculate Heart of Mary Statue, Basilica of Our Lady of Sorrows, Chicago.

CHAPTER 6
The Immaculate and Sorrowful Heart

In a loving invocation, Pope Julius II (1503-1513) exclaimed: "O most glorious Queen of mercy, I salute thy *virginal Heart, which remained free from all stain of sin.*"[48]

The Immaculate Conception
For a long time, theologians had great difficulty regarding the Immaculate Conception of the Blessed Virgin. How could one harmonize two seemingly contradictory truths of the faith: the universal mediation of Our Lord Jesus Christ, and Mary Most Holy's exemption from original sin? They argued: If she was free from original sin, then she did not need to be redeemed; but that would contradict the dogma of Christ's redemption of *all* the descendants of Adam.

That difficulty was overcome, however, by Franciscan theologians in the Middle Ages. In fact, the Blessed Virgin Mary was also redeemed by her Son, but in a different and unique way. While all other men were *cleansed* from sin through the merits of Jesus Christ, She was *exempted* from sin through those same merits. Thus, when applied to men in general, the Redemption was *liberating*, but when applied to the Mother of God, and only her, the Redemption was a *preserving* one. Both applications stem from the infinite merits of Christ, and are the fruit of His Incarnation, Passion, and Death for us on the Cross.

On proclaiming the dogma of the Immaculate Conception, Pope Pius IX (1846-1878) explained:

> "The most Holy Mother of God...by virtue of the *foreseen merits of Christ*, our Lord and Redeemer, was never subject to original sin, but was completely *preserved* from the original taint, and hence she was redeemed in a manner more sublime."[49]

---

[48] Cf. Hilario Marin, SJ, *El Corazón de Maria en el Magisterio de la Iglesia* (Madrid: Editorial Coculsa, 1960), 19. (Our translation.)

[49] Pius IX, Apostolic Constitution *Ineffabilis Deus* (The Immaculate Conception), Dec. 8, 1854, accessed May 18, 2016, http://www.papalencyclicals.net/Pius09/p9ineff.htm.

Immaculate, Full of Grace, Most Holy

For a creature, being free from any stain requires a most abundant grace. Even with the privilege of being exempted from original sin, remaining completely free from stain would not have been possible without extraordinary help from God. That is why the Archangel Gabriel greeted Mary saying she was "full of grace!" (Luke 1:28).

Being "full of grace" implies having taken sanctity to the highest degree of perfection. Mary is, thus, most holy.

These truths were beautifully expounded in the aforementioned Apostolic Constitution *Ineffabilis Deus*, issued by Pope Pius IX on December 8, 1854, when he proclaimed the dogma of the Immaculate Conception:

> When the Fathers and writers of the Church meditated on the fact that the most Blessed Virgin was, in the name and by order of God himself, proclaimed full of grace (cf. Luke 1:28) by the Angel Gabriel when he announced her most sublime dignity of Mother of God, they thought that this singular and solemn salutation, never heard before, showed that the Mother of God is the seat of all divine graces and is adorned with all gifts of the Holy Spirit. To them Mary is an almost infinite treasury, an inexhaustible abyss of these gifts, to such an extent that she was never subject to the curse and was, together with her Son, the only partaker of perpetual benediction. Hence she was worthy to hear Elizabeth, inspired by the Holy Spirit, exclaim: "Blessed are you among women, and blessed is the fruit of your womb" (cf. Luke 1:42). Hence, it is the clear and unanimous opinion of the Fathers that the most glorious Virgin, for whom "he who is mighty has done great things," was resplendent with such an abundance of heavenly gifts, with such a fullness of grace and with such innocence, that she is an unspeakable miracle of God—indeed, the crown of all miracles and truly the Mother of God; that she approaches as near to God himself as is possible for a created being; and that she is above all men and angels in glory.[50]

The Immaculate Heart of Mary symbolizes, therefore, the most sublime innocence and sanctity of Mary Most Holy, signifying her total fidelity to God.

---

[50] Ibid.

Sorrowful Heart

The Immaculate Heart of Mary is also a sorrowful one, pierced with grief. Not long after the joys of the Savior's birth, He was presented in the Temple. Turning to the Mother of God, the old Simeon prophesied: "Behold this child is set for the fall, and for the resurrection of many in Israel, and for a sign which shall be contradicted; *and thy own soul a sword shall pierce*, that, out of many hearts, thoughts may be revealed" (Luke 2:34-35).

Father Maximo Peinador, CMF, writes:

> The text mentions the soul. But ancient commentators such as Origen, Eutichius and others already speak about the Virgin's Heart. And the Christian people have understood it to represent the sorrowful Virgin with her Heart pierced by one or seven swords, symbols of her sorrows. And sorrow is the human feeling most attributed to the heart, both in the Scriptures and in literature.
>
> What were the feelings of the Heart of Mary as she heard Simeon's words? They are easy to guess: her admiration and joy at her Son's Presentation suddenly turn into bitter sorrow. Simeon's words were clear and peremptory not only as regards the future of the child but her own.... When were those words fulfilled? The Gospel narration, and especially that of Saint John, leave no doubt about it. Christ becomes a sign of contradiction as soon as He announces the new doctrine and performs His first miracles....
>
> But the full and definitive fulfillment of Simeon's announcement would take place on Calvary.... There, as nowhere else, Christ crucified was to be a sign of contradiction.... At the foot of the cross, His Mother would feel the prophesied sword pierce all the fibers of Her maternal Heart, with full force.[51]

Commenting on this passage of Scripture, the Church Fathers, including Saint Jerome, explain that Mary Most Holy was truly a martyr, having suffered in her soul all the torments of the Passion and Death of her Son.

Saint Jerome writes:

---

[51] Peinador, *Teologia Biblica*, 123-125. (Our translation.)

[B]ecause she suffered spiritually and more dreadfully by the sword of Christ's passion, she was more than a martyr. Hence it is evident that, since she loved more than all others, she, therefore, also suffered more, so much so that the force of the sorrow passed entirely through her soul and possessed it, in testimony to her exceptional love; because she suffered mentally, she was more than a martyr. Truly, her love was stronger than death, because she made Christ's death her own.[52]

The Seven Sorrows of the Heart of Mary

In 1815, Pope Pius VII (1800-1823) approved this beautiful prayer invoking the Seven Sorrows of the Heart of Mary:

1. I grieve for you, O Mary, most sorrowful, in the affliction of your tender heart at the prophecy of the holy and aged Simeon. Dear Mother, by your heart so afflicted, obtain for me the virtue of humility and the gift of the holy fear of God.

2. I grieve for you, O Mary most sorrowful, in the anguish of your most affectionate heart during the flight into Egypt and your sojourn there. Dear Mother, by your heart so troubled, obtain for me the virtue of generosity, especially toward the poor, and the gift of piety.

3. I grieve for you, O Mary most sorrowful, in those anxieties which tried your troubled heart at the loss of your dear Jesus. Dear Mother, by your heart so full of anguish, obtain for me the virtue of chastity and the gift of knowledge.

4. I grieve for you, O Mary most sorrowful, in the consternation of your heart at meeting Jesus as He carried His cross. Dear Mother, by your heart so troubled, obtain for me the virtue of patience and the gift of fortitude.

5. I grieve for you, O Mary most sorrowful, in the martyrdom which

---

[52] Thomas W. Mossman, trans., *The Great Commentary of Cornelius à Lapide, The Holy Gospel according Saint Mark [and] Saint Luke*, rev. Michael J. Miller (Fitzwilliam, N.H.: Loreto Publications, 2008), 284.

your generous heart endured in standing near Jesus in His agony. Dear Mother, by your afflicted heart, obtain for me the virtue of temperance and the gift of counsel.

6. I grieve for you, O Mary most sorrowful, in the wounding of your compassionate heart when the side of Jesus was struck by the lance before His Body was removed from the cross. Dear Mother, by your heart thus transfixed, obtain for me the virtue of fraternal charity and the gift of understanding.

7. I grieve for you, O Mary most sorrowful, for the pangs that wrenched your most loving heart at the burial of Jesus. Dear Mother, by your heart sunk in the bitterness of desolation, obtain for me the virtue of diligence and the gift of wisdom.[53]

---

[53] *The Seven Dolors of the Blessed Virgin Mary*, accessed Mar. 14, 2016, http://www.ewtn.com/library/MARY/DOLORS.htm.

America Needs Fatima protests against the blasphemous play *The Testament of Mary* by Colm Tóibín in New York City (April, 2013).

CHAPTER 7
The Wise and Immaculate Heart

Saint Luke the Evangelist, according to some commentators, heard the facts of the Annunciation and the childhood of Jesus directly from the Blessed Mother. Twice he refers to Our Lady's Heart as the center of her interior life: "But Mary kept all these words, *pondering them in her heart*" (Luke 2:19). "And he went down with them and came to Nazareth and was subject to them. And his mother *kept all these words in her heart*"(Luke 2:51).

Mary Meditated in her Heart
As Father Maximo Peinador aptly points out, Saint Luke's repeated observation that Mary kept these words and pondered them in her Heart "indicate the norm of the Virgin's interior life: meditation on the words and works of her Divine Son."[54]

Why did she meditate "in her heart"?

The expression seems to point to the Blessed Mother's contemplative side. She pondered with love. She reflected continually on the sublime mystery of God made man, while at the same time heartily uniting herself to the redemptive purpose of the Incarnation.

Here we enter the core of Marian spirituality, which is the loving contemplation of the mysteries of the Incarnation, Passion, and Death of the Immaculate Lamb.

In Mary, this contemplation assumed the tremendous quality of being the contemplative love of both a creature for her God and a Mother for her Son.

The Shepherds' Visit
Let us look at the context in which Saint Luke makes his first

---

[54] Peinador, *Teologia Biblica*, 41-2. (Our translation.)

reference to the Heart of Mary. It was at the Savior's birth, after the visit of the shepherds:

> And suddenly there was with the angel a multitude of the heavenly army, praising God, and saying: Glory to God in the highest; and on earth peace to men of good will. And it came to pass, after the angels departed from them into heaven, the shepherds said one to another: Let us go over to Bethlehem, and let us see this word that is come to pass, which the Lord hath showed to us.

> And they came with haste; and they found Mary and Joseph, and the infant lying in the manger. And seeing, they understood the word that had been spoken to them concerning this child. And all that heard, wondered; and at those things that were told them by the shepherds. *But Mary kept all these words, pondering them in her heart.* And the shepherds returned, glorifying and praising God, for all the things they had heard and seen, as it was told unto them (Luke 2:13-20).

Even amid the joys of the Savior's birth and His first glorification by the shepherds, Mary Most Holy does not interrupt her enduring role as a contemplative and "wise virgin" (cf. Matt. 25:1-13). She strives to understand the meaning of all things, contrasts this knowledge with everything that she knows from faith, and nourishes and strengthens her faith as she makes her judgments.

The Loss of the Child Jesus and His Finding in the Temple
The context for Saint Luke's second quote is the loss and finding of the Child Jesus in the Temple:

> And it came to pass, that, after three days, they found him in the temple, sitting in the midst of the doctors, hearing them, and asking them questions. And all that heard him were astonished at his wisdom and his answers. And seeing him, they wondered. And his mother said to him: "Son, why hast thou done so to us? Behold thy father and I have sought thee sorrowing." And he said to them: "How is it that you sought me? Did you not know, that I must be about my father's business?" And they understood not the word that he spoke unto them.

And he went down with them, and came to Nazareth, and was subject to them. *And his mother kept all these words in her heart.* And Jesus advanced in wisdom, and age, and grace with God and men" (Luke 2:46-52).

Here is how Saint Bede (673-735) comments on this passage:

The Virgin, whether she understood or whether she could not yet understand, equally laid up all things in her heart for reflection and diligent examination. Hence it follows, *And, his mother laid up all these things....* Mary the wisest of mothers, Mary *the mother of true wisdom,* becomes the scholar or disciple of the Child. For she yielded to Him not as to a boy, nor as to a man, but as unto God. Further, she pondered upon both His divine words and works, so that nothing that was said or done by Him was lost upon her, but as the Word itself was before in her womb, so now she conceived the ways and words of the same, and in a manner nursed them in her heart. And while indeed she thought upon one thing at the time, another she wanted to be more clearly revealed to her; and this was her constant rule and law through her whole life. It follows, and Jesus increased in wisdom.[55]

The Wise and Immaculate Heart

For Mary Most Holy, to "ponder in her heart" all things related to her Son meant that she not only reflected on them, but did so with love. She considered them not only with her mind but also with her heart, lovingly. Therefore, it is natural and legitimate that we see the Immaculate Heart of Mary as also being wise and full of wisdom.

"The Wise and Immaculate Heart of Mary," says Plinio Corrêa de Oliveira, "is an expression of Our Lady's wise and immaculate mentality. And among other things, it also expresses her ineffable goodness, sweetness, and inexhaustible mercy."[56]

---

[55] In Saint Thomas Aquinas, *The Catena Aurea Gospel of Saint Luke,* accessed July 12, 2016, http://dhspriory.org/thomas/english/CALuke.htm.

[56] Plinio Corrêa de Oliveira, "The Queenship of Our Lady and the Wise and Immaculate Heart of Mary," Lecture, May 31, 1975, accessed Feb. 26, 2016, http://www.pliniocorreadeoliveira.info/ DIS_SD_750531_Sapiencial_Coracao_de_Maria.htm#.VtC4vNAwCZM.

Every year, America Needs Fatima delivers large bouquets of roses to Fatima on the anniversary of the Miracle of the Sun. Each rose represents a Rosary Rally Captain who committed to gathering a group of people to pray the rosary in a public location in the United States of America. In 2016, there were 16,323 rosary rallies.

CHAPTER 8
Devotion to the Immaculate Heart of Mary

The direct object of this devotion is the person of Our Lady and is, thus, indistinguishable from general devotion to Mary. Its unique nature, however, lies in its *specific* object which is the Blessed Mother's *love for us*, her children.

Devotion in General

Saint Thomas Aquinas teaches that devotion is the will to give oneself readily to the service of God and to unite oneself entirely to Him. The essence of devotion is love and it is a fruit of the love of God. Devotion is powered by a twofold consideration of the Divine perfection: God's love for us and our need of this love given our extreme weakness in all things.

Given our human condition, things that we can observe with our senses excite more devotion than abstract ones. In practical terms, meditating on Christ's Humanity stimulates our love more than abstract principles.

In general, our devotion is for God, but we can also have devotion for creatures. As the Angelic Doctor teaches, "Devotion to God's holy ones, dead or living, does not terminate in them, but passes on to God, in so far as we honor God in His servants."[57]

Love is the essence of devotion. It stimulates and gives meaning to our acts of piety. For us to effectively love God and the saints we must seek to identify with them for "the beloved is like a part of ourselves."[58]

Thus, devotion should not just lead us to adoration and veneration, and to the service of God and the saints, but it should help us *imitate* them as much as possible.

---

[57] *Summa Theologica*, II-II, q. 82.

[58] *Sententia libri Ethicorum*, lib. 8 l. 1 n. 6.

Devotion to the Immaculate Heart

Devotion to the Heart of Mary is a very special kind of veneration, service, and imitation of the virtues of the Immaculate Heart.

The basis for this devotion should be unlimited confidence in the goodness and mercy of that Heart. This is essential as confidence is a condition for the practice of any virtue, including the virtue of religion which is the parent virtue of devotion.[59]

a) Confidence

Confidence draws us closer to Mary Most Holy. It diminishes or eliminates, as it were, the distance between our littleness and misery and the indescribable perfection of the Queen of Heaven. A child relies on his mother even when she is clothed in all the glory of power, as in the case of a queen or empress. The smaller and weaker the child—in fact, the more helpless he is—the more he leans on and feels supported by his mother.

When Mary agreed to become the Mother of God, she agreed to be our spiritual mother, too. The perfect love she has for her Son, Who came to redeem us, is joined to His love in offering His life for us.

Devotion to the Immaculate Heart is a devotion to Mary Most Holy that takes into account the special maternal love she has for us. In this devotion, we love "the mother of fair love, and of fear, and of knowledge, and of holy hope."[60]

Father L. Brien, SJ, writes:

> The Heart of Mary is a *virgin Heart*: faithful to the divine love that first conquered it, and wishing no other love. The Heart of Mary is a *Mother's Heart*: always accessible, capable of all forgiveness, continuously attentive to our needs, present wherever there is sorrow to console or a smile to give. The Heart of Mary is a *Queen's Heart*: as rich as it is good, as powerful as it is sweet; it can give us, or obtain for us, everything.[61]

---

[59] *Summa Theologica*, II-II, q. 82; q. 129, a. 6, ad 3.

[60] Sirach, 24:24.

[61] L. Brien, S. J., "La dévotion au Cœur Immaculé de Marie," in *Par Marie à la Céleste Patrie*, Synthèse de la Théologie (Montréal: Éditions de l'Institut Pie-XI, 1956), Vol. VIII, 127-8. (Our translation.)

b) Strength and Virtue

On our own, we are unable to correct our faults, maintain fidelity to the Catholic faith, or practice the virtues required in the face of today's widespread evil. However, supported by this Sovereign Queen, and drawing all the strength we need from her Immaculate Heart, we can correct our faults and practice these virtues.

Father Brien continues:

> Most pure, holy, *immaculate*, these are the best-known adjectives. At *Fatima*, the Virgin chose the latter as the one best suited to her Heart and that more fully corresponds to our needs. Indeed, the powerfully purifying Immaculate Heart of Mary could wash a thousand worlds of their worst filth; at the same time beautiful and attractive, it can raise thousands of virgins where evil dominates. Thus, heeding the message from Heaven [at Fatima] the Church designated it as the only sovereign hope, the universal salvation for our troubled and soiled times.[62]

c) Imitation

In the words of Prof. Plinio Corrêa de Oliveira,

> Only with Our Lady's help can we imitate her example. Devotion to Our Lady can only be acquired with her help. What better devotion to Mary Most Holy could we ask for than love of God and hatred of the devil, but also that holy integrity in loving good and hating evil, in a word, that holy intransigence that shines so much in her Immaculate Conception?[63]

d) Fighting for Our Lady

Thanks to the feudal mentality, the beautiful expression, "*Our Lady,*" appeared in the Middle Ages. It became common especially in France where Our Lady—*Notre Dame*—was the name given to the magnificent cathedral of Paris. It also spread to

---

[62] Ibid. (Our translation.)

[63] Plinio Corrêa de Oliveira, "Holy Intransigence, an Aspect of the Immaculate Conception," *Catolicismo*, No. 45, Sept. 1954. (Our translation.)

other countries, becoming *Madonna* (or *Mia Donna*, My Lady), in Italy; Our Lady, in England; *Nuestra Señora*, in Spain, and *Nossa Senhora* in Portugal.

Part of this feudal mentality was the understanding that a knight should serve his lady and defend her honor.

Should we not do this today as well? If we are devoted to the Immaculate Heart, should we not defend Our Lady's honor when she is insulted and offended by blasphemous art exhibits, movies, plays, shows, and novels? If devotion entails service, as in the case of a knight serving his lady, is this not the first service we should render Our Lady? Do we not have the duty of love to stand up for her and publicly express our protest and indignation when she is the target of debauched and sacrilegious mockery?

e) Apostolate

As previously mentioned, the essence of devotion is love. By its nature, love is effusive; love is expansive. If we are devoted to the Immaculate Heart, should not our love lead us to do everything we can to bring others to love the Immaculate Heart too? Should we not explain this devotion to those who do not know it? Should we not shape the world and society so that it is the "image and likeness"[64] of the Immaculate Heart? We certainly ought to do things that bring public honor to the Immaculate Heart. By doing so, we will labor to bring about the fulfillment of Our Lord's Prayer "Thy kingdom come, Thy will be done, on earth, as it is in heaven."[65]

Finally, our devotion to the Immaculate Heart must have all the characteristics of an authentic devotion as taught by Saint Louis de Montfort.

---

[64] Gen. 1:26.

[65] Matt. 6:10.

Saint Louis-Marie Grignion de Montfort:
Signs of Authentic Devotion to Our Lady

After having laid bare and condemned the false devotions to the most holy Virgin, we must, in a few words, characterize the true devotion. It must be (1) interior, (2) tender, (3) holy, (4) constant, and (5) disinterested.

True devotion to our Lady is *interior*, that is to say, it comes from the spirit and the heart. It flows from the esteem we have of her, the high idea we have formed of her greatness, and the love which we have for her.

It is *tender*, that is to say, full of confidence in her, like a child's confidence in his loving Mother. This confidence makes the soul have recourse to her in all its bodily or mental necessities, with much simplicity, trust, and tenderness. It implores the aid of its good Mother, at all times, in all places, and above all things; in its doubts, that it may be enlightened; in its wanderings, that it may be brought back into the right path; in its temptations, that it may be supported; in its weaknesses, that it may be strengthened; in its falls, that it may be lifted up; in its discouragements, that it may be cheered; in its scruples, that they may be taken away; in its crosses, toils, and disappointments of life, that it may be consoled under them. In a word, in all its evils of body and mind, the soul's ordinary refuge is in Mary, without fearing to be importunate to her or to displease Jesus Christ.

True devotion is *holy*, that is to say, it leads the soul to avoid sin, and to imitate in the Blessed Virgin particularly her profound humility, her lively faith, her blind obedience, her continual prayer, her universal mortification, her divine purity, her ardent charity, her heroic patience, her angelical sweetness, and her divine wisdom. These are the ten principal virtues of the most holy Virgin.

True devotion to our Lady is *constant*. It confirms the soul in good, and does not let it easily abandon its spiritual exercises. It makes it courageous in opposing the world in its fashions and maxims, the flesh in its wearinesses and passions, and the devil in his temptations. So that a person truly devout to our Blessed Lady is neither changeable, irritable, scrupulous nor timid. It is not that such a person does not fall, or change sometimes in the sensible feeling of devotion, or in the amount of devotion itself. But when he falls, he rises again by stretching out his hand to his good Mother. If he loses the taste and relish of devotion, he does not disturb himself because of that; for the just and faithful client of Mary lives on the faith of Jesus and Mary, and not on sentiments and sensibilities.

Lastly, true devotion to our Blessed Lady is *disinterested*, that is to say, it inspires the soul not to seek itself but God only, and God in His holy Mother. A true client of Mary does not serve that august Queen from a spirit of lucre and interest, nor for its own good, whether temporal, corporal, or spiritual; but exclusively because she merits to be served, and God alone in her. He does not love her precisely because she does him good or because he hopes in her; but because she is so worthy of love. It is on this account that he loves and serves her as faithfully in his disgust and dryness, as in his sweetness and sensible fervor. He loves her as much on Calvary, as at the marriage of Cana. Oh! how such a client of our Blessed Lady, who has no self-seeking in his service of her, is agreeable and precious in the eyes of God and his holy Mother! But in these days how rare is such a sight! It is that it may be less rare that I have taken my pen to put on paper what I have taught, in public and in private, during my missions for many years.[66]

---

[66] Saint Louis de Montfort, *True Devotion to Mary* (Spring Grove, Penn.: The American Society for the Defense of Tradition, Family, and Property, 2013), 45-6.

Every year in January, America Needs Fatima joins the March for Life in Washington, D.C. Some weeks before the March, the names of those who will not be able to attend the March are collected. These names are printed on a large banner and carried during the March for Life.

CHAPTER 9
Consecration to the Immaculate Heart of Mary

One of the most excellent forms of devotion to Our Lady is consecrating oneself to her as Saint Louis Grignion de Montfort advocated with great zeal. As he says in his book *True Devotion to Mary*, and as is attested by Church scholars, this was already an ancient practice in the Church.

What Is "Consecration"?

According to the *Catholic Encyclopedia*,

> Consecration, in general, is an act by which a thing is separated from a common and profane to a sacred use, or by which a person or thing is dedicated to the service and worship of God by prayers, rites, and ceremonies. The custom of consecrating persons to the Divine service and things to serve in the worship of God may be traced to the remotest times.[67]

Personal consecration, Father Joseph de Finance, SJ, explains, is the act of giving oneself to God. Taken in its etymological sense (from the Latin *sacrum facere*, to make sacred) it can be called a sacrifice. In this regard, Saint Augustine writes in the *City of God*: "Man himself, consecrated in the name of God and given to God, is a sacrifice to the extent that he dies to the world in order to live for God."[68]

Consecration can be *official* when done by a qualified minister who accepts it on the Church's behalf, or *private* when it is simply a manifestation of a person's own will to confide an object—or himself—to God in order to receive His protection.

Official consecrations include the Sacraments of Baptism, Confirmation, and Holy Orders.

---

[67] A. J. Schulte, "Consecration," in *The Catholic Encyclopedia*, Vol. IV (New York: Robert Appleton Company, 1908).

[68] This whole section is based on Father Joseph de Finance, SJ, "Consécration," in *Dictionnaire de Spiritualité*, Vol. II, cols. 1575-1583.

Every baptized person is consecrated since he receives a special sign from God that establishes a new, supernatural relationship between the creature and his Creator. Baptism is the fundamental consecration from which all others derive. Confirmation is a consecration that marks us with a seal of the Holy Ghost to fight for Christ and His Church. The sacrament of Holy Orders is a very special consecration, a more direct participation in Our Lord's Priesthood.

Finally, in the official or public sphere, the religious consecration with vows is officially accepted by the Church through religious institutions.

A private consecration is an act by which a person commits himself to live his self-offering to God or his surrender to Our Lady in a more profound and all-encompassing manner. It is not, however, a vow, like the religious vows made in Institutes of Consecrated Life (orders, congregations, secular institutes, and so on).

To Whom Is the Consecration Made?

"The answer to this question seems obvious: to God alone," Father de Finance writes. "Only God is entitled to own us entirely.... Indeed, a person is made sacred only by belonging to God; hence, to consecrate is, by definition, to consecrate to God."

About Our Lady, he notes, one can speak of an effective, though analogical, consecration. It is consecration in a secondary sense and subordinated to the consecration to Christ.

Indeed, Our Lord and Our Lady are not two distinct principles in our spiritual life. By the will of God, they form a single life-giving principle. Our Lady participates in the universal Redemption of Christ in such a way that she is our mother in what is most precious to us: divine grace. She is the Mother of Divine Grace. So the consecration to Mary Most Holy is subordinate to the consecration to Our Lord Jesus Christ, as Saint

Louis de Montfort explains in his *True Devotion*. He teaches that to consecrate oneself to Mary Most Holy is nothing other than the most excellent way of consecrating oneself to Our Lord Jesus Christ.

As for the saints, Father de Finance says, a consecration to one of them is simply an act of homage rendered to a heavenly protector. It is a stronger form of devotion, but it is not a true consecration in the theological sense of the word.

Consecration of Countries

Father José Maria Canal, CMF, points out that just as an individual can consecrate himself to God or to the Blessed Virgin Mary to serve them better, so also dioceses, parishes, towns, families, and even countries can be consecrated by their official representatives.

He writes,

> Besides a private offering, one can also speak of a public offering, that is, the act a superior performs by dedicating his subjects to God's service.... But in a public consecration, it is paramount that the superior's act represent the desire and intention of his subjects; and that the latter be closely united to their leader's intention so that they are collectively conscious of the act. The effectiveness and value of this public act depends on the greater or lesser consonance of individuals with the leader's will. As such, a public offering is an act of religion.[69]

The Pope's Power to Consecrate Non-Catholic Countries

Based on the preceding premises, it is easy to understand the legitimacy of a bishop consecrating his diocese, or a president or king consecrating his country to the Sacred Heart—as done by Ecuador's President Garcia Moreno in 1873—or to Our Lady—as civil and religious authorities jointly did in several countries in the first half of the twentieth century.[70]

---

[69] Canal, *Consagración*, Vol. II, 17-8.

[70] Cf. Ibid., Vols. I and II.

But what about a non-Catholic country such as Russia, whose consecration to the Immaculate Heart of Mary was requested by Our Lady at Fatima? Can this be done?

This problem was solved by Pope Leo XIII (1878-1903) in the Encyclical *Annum Sacrum* (1899), in which he announced the consecration of the human race to the Sacred Heart of Jesus. Christ is the King of all men by right and by conquest, the Sovereign Pontiff teaches. He is king even of those rebellious subjects who revolted against His law and His Church. He is King even of those that ignore them. The Pope says:

> This world-wide and solemn testimony of allegiance and piety is especially appropriate to Jesus Christ, who is the Head and Supreme Lord of the [human] race. His empire extends not only over Catholic nations and those who, having been duly washed in the waters of Holy Baptism, belong of right to the Church, although erroneous opinions keep them astray, or dissent from her teaching cuts them off from her care; it comprises also all those who are deprived of the Christian faith, so that the whole human race is most truly under the power of Jesus Christ.[71]

Leo XIII explains that this act of consecration will attract special graces to all, making Catholics more fervent, and bringing light and help for the conversion of non-Catholics.

Since Our Lord has this universal empire over all peoples and nations, then the Pope as His Vicar can consecrate even non-Catholic nations in His Name.

---

[71] Leo XIII, Enc. *Annum Sacrum*, no. 3.

Interior Dispositions to
Consecrate Oneself to Our Lady

The act of consecration to Our Lady requires some interior dispositions which Prof. Plinio Corrêa de Oliveira summarizes as follows:

The person should:

1. Formally renounce everything that makes him incompatible with the Blessed Virgin, that is, all sins, heresies or laxity in the practice of the Faith;

2. Make a resolution to honor, serve, and glorify Our Lady in a special way;

3. Beg her to accept these dispositions and cover with special assistance the person thus consecrating himself to her.

Thus, in the consecration, we make a *negative resolution*: To refrain from doing anything *against* the one to whom we consecrate ourselves. And the consecration has a *positive resolution*: To do everything we can *for* her. And we say a prayer: That she accept this offering and grant us, in turn, her special protection.

None of this is purely symbolic, without consequences in reality. When seriously thought out, desired and executed, this is an act of transcendental gravity. Because of this, an act of consecration should be done with maturity and reflection, for *doing it frivolously and carelessly would be taking the holy name of God in vain*. Literally. The consecration is something most serious on our part, and it is taken even more so by Our Lady.[72]

---

[72] Plinio Corrêa de Oliveira, "Consecration to Our Lady," *Legionário*, No. 675, July 15, 1945.

CHAPTER 10
Consecration of Russia

Sister Lúcia asked Our Lord why He did not convert Russia without having the Pope consecrate that country to the Immaculate Heart of Mary. He answered: "Because I want My whole Church to acknowledge that consecration as a triumph of the Immaculate Heart of Mary, so that it may extend devotion to it and place devotion to this Immaculate Heart beside the devotion to My Sacred Heart."[73]

Context of Devotion to the Immaculate Heart of Mary
Thus, the consecration of Russia requested by God is in the context of devotion to the Immaculate Heart. Our Lady said in her 1929 request: "The moment has arrived wherein God is asking the Holy Father, in union with all the bishops of the world, to consecrate Russia to my Immaculate Heart. He promises to save it by this means."

The request that the consecration be made by the Holy Father and all the world's bishops in union with him supposes that a universal preparation be done beforehand to spread and explain the devotion to the Immaculate Heart of Mary.

This consecration and the conversion of Russia resulting from it are intended by God to be a triumph of the Immaculate Heart of Mary that will help spread this devotion even more.

The very fact that Our Lady asked for the Communion of Reparation to her Immaculate Heart *before* requesting the consecration of Russia is a further indication of how much the devotion to the Immaculate Heart is the context for this consecration.

"If My Requests Are Fulfilled, Russia Will Convert"
Later on, we will see how a careful reading of Our Lady's words to Sister Lúcia in the so-called second part of the Secret, as well

---

[73] Sister Lúcia's letter to her confessor—May 18, 1936.

as heavenly communications the same seer received later, make it clear that the consecration should have been done *before* World War II to obtain the promised effect.[74]

Here we need to deal with another aspect of the issue: Mary Most Holy promised that "If my requests [Communion of Reparation and Consecration of Russia] are fulfilled, *Russia will convert.*"

What is the conversion of a person or country?

Since the conversion of a country depends on the conversion of its people, let us first consider what individual conversion entails.

True Conversion Requires True Faith

As Father Benedict Guldner, SJ, explains when dealing with conversion, both the Natural Law and the Divine Law require man to seek the truth and the true religion and adhere to them:

> Every man is bound by the natural law to seek the true religion, embrace it when found, and conform his life to its principles and precepts. And it is a dogma of the Church defined by the Vatican Council [First Vatican Council, 1870] that man is able by the natural light of reason to arrive at the certain knowledge of the existence of the one true God, our Creator and Lord. The same council teaches that faith is a gift of God necessary for salvation, that it is an act of the intellect commanded by the will, and that it is a supernatural act.... *[T]he duty of embracing the true religion is of natural and positive Divine right.*[75]

Pope Pius XII, in the Encyclical *Mystici Corporis Christi* (1943), and the Holy Office in a letter to the Archbishop of Boston (1949) teach that belonging to the Church is necessary for salvation, or at least that the person be related to the Church by an implicit desire to adhere to her and to accept everything that she teaches. This second situation occurs when a person is in the state of *invincible ignorance* having no

---

[74] See Appendix I, page 83.

[75] Benedict Guldner, "Conversion," in *The Catholic Encyclopedia*, Vol. IV (New York: Robert Appleton Company, 1908).

adequate means to know Catholic doctrine. Analyzing this point in his treatise *On the Church of Jesus Christ,* Father Joaquín Salaverri lists a series of papal and conciliar documents through the ages that affirm the need to belong to the Church, at least in desire, to save one's soul. He concludes: "*Dogmatic value*: One clearly sees through the documents of the Church that the need to belong to the Church is a *dogma of faith.*"[76]

Therefore, speaking of a conversion of Russia as promised by Our Lady at Fatima implies that at least a very considerable part of the population join the Catholic Church.

Consecration: a Way of Living the Faith

In his book, *Consecration to the Virgin and Her Heart,* Father José M. Canal, CMF, explains that consecration requires a lively adhesion to the faith:

> "A consecration may not be perfect if a positive element, that is, earnestness or adhesion [to the Faith] is not joined by a negative element, that is, renunciation [of sin]. If the baptized person renounces sin and dies with Christ, he does so to live a new life, to become 'a new creature' (Gal. 6:15)."

He goes on to explain that, according to Saint Thomas, the Faith "purifies our hearts" paving the way for charity and hope, and at the same time illuminates our intellect to see God as our ultimate end.

"In this sense," he says, "faith is the principle of our adhesion to God, since neither hope nor charity, rooted in the will, can attain their goal if one's intellect does not present it to them."

One of the means to enkindle this virtue, Father Canal concludes, "is to avoid sin, which obfuscates understanding and

---

[76] Joaquín Salaverri, SJ, *De la Iglesia de Jesucristo*, Vol. III in *Suma de la Sagrada Teología Escolástica*, Padres de la Compañía de Jesús, eds., Book 3, ch. 2, art. 5, accessed July 12, 2016, http://www.mercaba.org/TEOLOGIA/STE/iglesia/libro_3_cap_2.htm#Articulo%20V.

imprisons the heart. The star of faith cannot shine in the swamp of lust."[77]

Conversion of Russia to the True Faith

The conversion of Russia that Our Lady promised as part and parcel of the triumph of her Immaculate Heart therefore implies: 1) conversion to the true Faith and 2) allegiance to the only Church of Christ, the Holy Roman Catholic Church, on a scale large enough to warrant the statement that Russia has become a Catholic country.

Since this conversion is one of the elements of the triumph of the Immaculate Heart of Mary, it must show the marks of that triumph: living faith, ardent charity, unfailing hope.

Plinio Corrêa de Oliveira writes,

> When the Church promotes the consecration of nations, dioceses, families or peoples to the Sacred Heart of Jesus or the Immaculate Heart of Mary, it intends for the creatures so consecrated to formulate the resolution of belonging particularly to the Heart of Jesus or the Heart of Mary, more faithfully obeying their laws, taking them more perfectly as models, and, conversely, receiving their specific and vigilant attention in a special way. Thus, the consecration is not a mere rite, a vague formula to be recited at a time of pious emotion. It is above all a reflected, deliberate, voluntary and profound act which implies the resolve to have a more perfect integration in the doctrine and life of the Holy Catholic Church, which is the only real way to belong to Jesus and Mary.[78]

Thus, the whole social life of a country needs to reflect this. For all these reasons, we cannot say that Russia has converted. Despite the fall of communism, the majority of Russians are still schismatic. On the moral plane, Russia has one of the highest abortion rates in the world.

---

[77] Canal, *Consagración*, Vol. II, 93-4.

[78] Plinio Corrêa de Oliveira, "The Consecration to the Immaculate Heart of Mary," Ave Maria (São Paulo), No. 31, July 1943, accessed Feb. 27, 2016, http://www.pliniocorreadeoliveira.info/ OUT%20-%20194307_A%20Consagra%C3%A7%C3%A3o%20ao%20Imaculado%20Cora%C3 %A7%C3%A3o%20de%20Maria.htm.

We Belong to God by Nature

From the earliest days of the Church, chosen souls, recognizing the total submission owed to God as our Creator, Redeemer, and Sanctifier, considered themselves His slaves.

Thus, in the early centuries of Christianity, **Saint Agatha**, facing martyrdom under the persecution of Decius (250-253) proudly confessed her faith by proclaiming, "I am a slave of Christ;" **Saint Maximus Martyr** (circa 250 A.D.) said: "I was born free, but am a servant of Christ."

Often, because of the intimate union existing between Mary Most Holy and her Divine Son in the work of Redemption, many of these souls declared themselves slaves not only of God, but also of Our Lady.

Saint Ildephonsus of Toledo (607-669) wrote:

> For this reason [I am] thy servant [O Mary] because thy Son is my Lord. And I am a slave of my Lord's servant, for thou, my Lady, wert made Mother of thy Lord.... I make myself a slave of His Mother to be a devoted slave of the Son thou hast begotten.

Saint Odilo of Cluny (962-1048) offered himself to Mary: "I surrender myself as thy slave;" and **Saint Bernard of Clairvaux** (1091-1153) stated: "I am a vile slave greatly honored to be a servant, both of the Son and the Mother."

From this saintly lineage arose **Saint Louis-Marie Grignion de Montfort** (1673-1716), who systematized and spread the slavery to Our Lady in his celebrated *True Devotion to Mary*.

In 1917, during the third Fatima apparition, Our Lady announced, "I will come to ask for the consecration of Russia to my Immaculate Heart." Her intention was to prevent World War II and the spreading of the errors of Russia.

CHAPTER 11
The Conversion of Russia and the Revolutionary Process

In her Fatima apparition on July 13, 1917, the Blessed Mother warned:

> If they listen to my requests, *Russia will be converted and there will be peace. If not, she will scatter her errors throughout the world,* provoking wars and persecutions of the Church. The good will be martyred, the Holy Father will have much to suffer and various nations will be annihilated.

Devotion to the Immaculate Heart and the Scourge of Communism

From the beginning, Fatima experts interpreted the "errors of Russia" as the communist ideology. None of them thought it referred to the theological errors of the "Russian Orthodox Church," as the capacity of the self-governing or national "autocephalous churches" to disseminate their errors is very small and usually restricted to emigrants from those nations.

The connection with the communist ideology becomes clearer when one considers the following: when Our Lady appeared, from May to October 1917, Russia had not yet been dominated by the Bolsheviks. Although the Russian Czar had already abdicated, and the country was in chaos at the time of the apparitions, the communists had still not seized power. The "moderate" Kerensky government fell, and the Bolsheviks took control only on November 7, 1917 (October 25 by the Julian calendar used in Russia).

It is interesting to note that in 1917 Our Lady did not ask for the consecration of Russia and for the Five First Saturdays devotion to honor her Immaculate Heart. She said: "To prevent it [the war and persecution of the Church], *I will come to ask* for the consecration of Russia to my Immaculate Heart and the

Communion of reparation on the first Saturdays."

The Blessed Virgin came to ask for the First Saturdays devotion of reparation on December 10, 1925, and for Russia's consecration on June 13, 1929.

How do we explain Our Lady's postponement of these two requests? Could it be because they would be more clearly understood if she made them later? And what else happened after her 1917 Fatima apparitions other than the seizure of power by the communists, their consolidation, and the beginning of communist expansion around the world?

Thus, devotion to the Immaculate Heart—whether expressed by the consecration of Russia or by the First Saturdays devotion—cannot be unrelated to the scourge of communism.

Errors of Russia? Or "Errors of the Revolution"?

To delve deeper into this topic, the communist ideology is only the most advanced stage of the historical process of moral decay in Christendom. This process began with the Renaissance and Protestantism, became more dynamic with the French Revolution of 1789, and culminated with communism. In his luminous essay *Revolution and Counter-Revolution,* Plinio Corrêa de Oliveira calls this process "the Revolution":

> This terrible enemy has a name: It is called the *Revolution.* Its profound cause is an explosion of pride and sensuality that has inspired, not one system, but, rather, a whole chain of ideological systems. Their wide acceptance gave rise to the three great revolutions in the history of the West: the Pseudo-Reformation, the French Revolution, and communism.[79]

Further on he quotes a description of this "terrible enemy" by Pope Pius XII:

> It [the "terrible enemy"] is to be found everywhere and among everyone; it can be both violent and astute. In these last centuries, it has attempted to disintegrate the intellectual, moral, and social

---

[79] Plinio Corrêa de Oliveira, *Revolution and Counter-Revolution* (York, Penn.: The American Society for the Defense of Tradition, Family, and Property, 1993), 3, accessed July 12, 2016, http://www.tfp.org/tfp-home/books/revolution-and-counter-revolution-v15-1370.html.

unity in the mysterious organism of Christ. It has sought nature without grace, reason without faith, freedom without authority, and, at times, authority without freedom. It is an "enemy" that has become more and more apparent with an absence of scruples that still surprises: Christ yes; the Church no! [Protestantism] Afterwards: God yes; Christ no! [Deism of the French Revolution] Finally the impious shout: God is dead and, even, God never existed! [Atheism of communism] And behold now the attempt to build the structure of the world on foundations which we do not hesitate to indicate as the main causes of the threat that hangs over humanity: economy without God, law without God, politics without God (Pius XII, Allocution to the Union of Men of the Italian Catholic Action, October 12, 1952).[80]

Now then, even Western countries that have not adopted Marxism as a philosophy of government or state capitalism as a political-economic system are rife with errors that lead to communism. These are errors of the Revolution. Accordingly, to be truly effective, the triumph of the Immaculate Heart promised by Our Lady at Fatima implies not only a defeat of communism but the entire Revolution leading up to it.

Just as at the time of the Pseudo-Reformation (which started in Germany in 1517), one could have said that "Germany will spread her errors throughout Europe," meaning the errors of Protestantism, so also, at Fatima, Our Lady said "[Russia] will spread her errors throughout the world," meaning the errors of communism.

Conversion of Russia, Conversion of the World
Plinio Corrêa de Oliveira believed that a conversion of Russia would hardly be possible without a conversion of the West as well. For otherwise, given the high permeability of the modern world, those Western errors and trends that lead to communism would negatively influence a converted Russia.

On other occasions, the same Catholic thinker made clear that he considered the triumph of the Immaculate Heart of

---

[80] Cf. Ibid., 13.

Mary, promised at Fatima, as a defeat of the Revolution.[81] Thus, in the 1950s, he wrote:

> The writings of Saint Louis Grignion de Montfort are full of prophetic insights (we employ these words with the full caution required by sound Catholic language) on the queenship of Mary most holy, such as the end of the era of catastrophes inaugurated with the Protestant Pseudo-Reformation. The royalty of Jesus Christ and the royalty of Mary Most Holy are not different things. The queenship of Mary is nothing but a means—or rather, the means—to the effective royalty of Jesus Christ. The Heart of Jesus reigns and triumphs in the kingdom and triumph of the Heart of Mary. The Heart of Mary's reign and triumph are nothing but the triumph and reign of the Heart of Jesus. These considerations cannot be unrelated to what the little shepherds heard from the Immaculate Heart of Mary at Fatima.[82]

In another article around the same time, he pondered:

> "In the end, my Immaculate Heart will triumph," the Virgin said on her third apparition at the Cova da Iria. Oh! Neo-paganism, a thousand times worse than ancient paganism, your days are numbered! The Soviet power will fall and the influence of the Revolution in the West will also crumble. Our Lady said so, and before her all the grandees of the earth and all princes of darkness are powerless.[83]

---

[81] Cf. Plinio Corrêa de Oliveira, "Dead? Or Red? The Great Crossroads of Our Times from the Standpoint of the Fatima Message," *Catolicismo*, No. 411, Mar. 1985.

[82] Plinio Corrêa de Oliveira, "Pius XII and the Era of Mary," *Catolicismo*, No. 48, Dec. 1954.

[83] Plinio Corrêa de Oliveira, "Hodie in Terra Canunt Angeli, Laetantur Archangeli, Hodie exultant Justi—The Voice of Fatima," *Catolicismo* No., 84, Dec. 1957.

CHAPTER 12
Revolution, Counter-Revolution and the Immaculate Heart

According to Plinio Corrêa de Oliveira, the Revolution "is an explosion of pride and sensuality," that inspired "a whole chain of ideological systems" that has been feeding the process of Christendom's destruction. Conversely, a movement opposed to the Revolution can be called the Counter-Revolution, which represents a restoration of order. [84]

Although we find ourselves at the apex of this process, we are absolutely certain of its defeat. It was guaranteed at Fatima by the promised triumph of the Immaculate Heart of Mary.

Here we shall analyze how devotion to the Immaculate Heart of Mary, indicated by Our Lady as the means to triumph, relates to and opposes pride and sensuality, the unbridled passions that fuel the Revolution.

Clashing Tendencies
a) Humility

Saint Teresa of Jesus defined humility as the truth.

She writes: "Once I was considering why Our Lord was so fond of this virtue of humility." And she went on to say that she understood through divine illumination that "since God is the supreme Truth, and humility *is to walk in truth*, it is crucial not to have ourselves in high regard but [to see that] we are misery and nothing; and he who does not understand that is living a lie."[85]

For his part, Saint Thomas Aquinas says that the truth of humility, "regards chiefly the subjection of man to God, for Whose

---

[84] Corrêa de Oliveira, *R-CR*, 3.

[85] Santa Teresa de Jesús, *Las Moradas*, Moradas Sextas Capítulo 10, n. 7, accessed Jan. 21, 2016 http://hjg.com.ar/teresa_moradas/moradas_6_10.html.

sake he humbles himself by subjecting himself to others."[86]

Humility is linked to the virtue of temperance which includes all virtues that restrain our disordered tendencies and appetites.

It gives, therefore, that mental balance whereby we make correct judgments about ourselves and others. It reduces our desires of grandeur to their due proportions according to our abilities and possibilities.

Humility is the foundation of the spiritual life because it makes the soul submissive to God, thus preparing the soul to receive divine grace. As Saint James put it, "God resists the proud, and gives his grace to the humble."[87]

Thanks to this adhesion to the truth, which is true submission to God, humility leads us to acquire wisdom. As the book of Proverbs explains: "Where humility is, there also is wisdom."[88]

One can conclude that humility is necessary to have the spirit of the Counter-Revolution.

b) Pride

Just as humility comes from a spirit of submission to God, pride, its opposite, comes from revolt against Him and from a desire to abandon our full dependence on Him. As the Prophet Jeremias says: "Thou hast broken My yoke, thou hast burst My bands, and thou says: '*I will not serve.*'"[89]

Saint Thomas says that "pride makes a man despise the Divine law." It removes the main obstacle to sin which is the fear of God. The proud person thus plunges not only into vice but also into error. The saint adds,

> [T]he proud man subjects not his intellect to God, that he may receive the knowledge of truth from Him, according to Matthew

---

[86] *Summa Theologica*, II-II, q. 161, a. 1, ad 5.

[87] James 4:6.

[88] Prov. 11:2. Cf. *Summa Theologica*, II-II, q. 162, a. 3, ad 1.

[89] Jeremiah 2:20. *Summa Theologica*, II-II, q. 162, a. 2.

11:25, "Thou hast hid these things from the wise and the prudent,"
i.e. from the proud, who are wise and prudent in their own eyes,
"and hast revealed them to little ones," i.e. to the humble.

Likewise, the Angelic Doctor continues, the proud person
does not want to learn from other men, as the Scripture says:
"If thou wilt incline thy ear, thou shalt receive instruction."[90]
"[T]he proud," Saint Thomas concludes, "through delighting in
their own excellence disdain the excellence of truth."[91]

We find the essence of the Revolution in the proud person's
scorn for the truth and the Divine Law.

c) Chastity v. Sensuality

Along with pride, the Revolution is driven by unbridled sensuality. Both pride and sensuality cause the person to rebel
against the Creator, Who imposes norms and limits. This re-
bellion against submission to God leads toward anarchism.[92]

The virtues of humility and chastity restrain these two tendencies and keep them within their proper limits.

Chastity is, so to speak, a form of corporal "humility" that
subjects our body to the laws of the Creator just as humility
subjects our minds. It moderates and guides the impulses of
concupiscence according to the order of reason. Saint Thomas
states that "Chastity takes its name from the fact that reason
'chastises' concupiscence, which, like a child, needs curbing."[93]

Although chastity operates on the body, it properly resides
in the soul, "[f]or it belongs to chastity that a man make moderate use of bodily members in accordance with the judgment
of his reason and the choice of his will."[94]

Like humility, it is linked to the virtue of temperance, which

---

[90] Sirach 6:34.

[91] *Summa Theologica*, II-II, q. 162, a. 3 ad 1.

[92] Cf. Corrêa de Oliveira, *R-CR*, 46-54.

[93] *Summa Theologica*, II-II, q. 151, a. 1.

[94] Ibid., ad. 1.

curtails our disordered impulses and subjects them to reason. Chastity frees us from the tyranny of lust, which Saint Thomas describes thus:

> When the lower powers are strongly moved towards their objects, the result is that the higher powers are hindered and disordered in their acts. Now the effect of the vice of lust is that the lower appetite, namely the concupiscible, is most vehemently intent on its object, to wit, the object of pleasure, on account of the vehemence of the pleasure. Consequently, the higher powers, namely the reason and the will, are most grievously disordered by lust.[95]

Lust darkens the intellect, weakens the faith, cools charity, distorts sentiment, leads to cynicism and duplicity, and drags us to other vices.

Humble Heart of Mary

The Sacred Heart of Jesus can be defined by the words of the Divine Redeemer: "I am meek and humble of heart."[96] His is a humble Heart, entirely submissive to the will of the Eternal Father.

The same can be said of the Immaculate Heart of Mary, as that Heart beat in unison with the Sacred Heart of Jesus. The Immaculate Heart of Mary is "meek and humble" and entirely submissive to the will of her Divine Son.

Saints and Fathers of the Church say that it was this humility that attracted the Word of God to the Blessed Virgin Mary resulting in the Incarnation.

Saint Augustine sums up that thought with a beautiful formula:

> O truly blessed humility of Mary, who brought forth the Lord to men, gave life to mortals, renewed the heavens, purified the world, opened paradise, and delivered the souls of men from hell.[97]

---

[95] Ibid., II-II, q. 153, a. 5.

[96] Matt. 11:29.

[97] Saint Alphonsus de Liguori, *The Glories of Mary* (New York: P. J. Kenedy & Sons, 1888), 598-9.

Likewise, Saint Alphonsus de Liguori, commenting on the Virgin's reply to the angel as he proposed that She become the Mother of God, writes:

> Oh powerful answer, which gave joy in heaven, and poured upon the earth a vast flood of graces and blessings! Answer, that hardly came forth from *the humble heart of Mary* before it drew from the bosom of the eternal Father, the only-begotten Son, to become man in her most pure womb! Yes, for hardly had she uttered these words: *Behold the handmaid of the Lord; be it done to me according to thy word;* when immediately the Word was made flesh: *Verbum caro factum est;* the Son of God became also the Son of Mary.[98]

Therefore, it is from devotion to the Humble Heart of Mary Most Holy that the forces capable of defeating the Revolution will spring forth.

Immaculate Heart of Mary

The humility of Our Lady's heart is a reflection of her immaculate purity. Having been conceived without original sin and receiving all the graces that a creature can receive and that pertain to the dignity of the Mother of God, not only was she free from sin but even from the tendency to sin resulting from the original fall.[99]

The Church applies to her the words from the Canticle of Canticles: "You are beautiful, my beloved, and there is no blemish in you."[100]

Saint Ephrem the Syrian (306-373) is at a loss for words to express the unfathomable purity of the Virgin of Virgins:

> Most holy Lady, Mother of God, alone most pure in soul and body, alone exceeding all perfection of purity...alone made in thy entirety

---

[98] Ibid., 416.

[99] Pius IX: "Therefore, far above all the angels and all the saints so wondrously did God endow her with the abundance of all heavenly gifts poured from the treasury of his divinity that this mother, ever absolutely free of all stain of sin, all fair and perfect, would possess that fullness of holy innocence and sanctity than which, under God, one cannot even imagine anything greater, and which, outside of God, no mind can succeed in comprehending fully." Apost. Const. *Ineffabilis.*

[100] Cant. 4:7.

the home of all the graces of the Most Holy Spirit, and hence exceed-ing beyond all compare even the angelic virtues in purity and sanc-tity of soul and body.... My Lady most holy, all-pure, all-immaculate, all-stainless, all-undefiled, all-incorrupt, all-inviolate spotless robe of Him Who clothes Himself with light as with a garment...flower un-fading, purple woven by God, alone most immaculate.[101]

As Saint Alphonsus de Liguori states in his *Glories of Mary*, many saints, including Saint Jerome and Saint Thomas Aquinas, believed that the extraordinary beauty of Mary Most Holy rather than exciting concupiscence in those who admired her, led to chastity instead.[102]

Devotion to the Immaculate Heart of Mary is, therefore, of paramount importance to combat the unbridled sensuality driving the Revolution.

Perfect for Our Times

Based on these considerations which are simply a quick sum-mary of what the saints and popes have said along the cen-turies, Our Lady at Fatima could not have provided a more appropriate devotion for our times than the devotion to her Immaculate Heart.

---

[101] Saint Ephrem the Syrian, *Precationes ad Deiparam in Opp. Graec. Lat.*, III, 524-37, in Holweck, F. "Immaculate Conception" in *The Catholic Encyclopedia* (New York: Robert Appleton Com-pany. 1910), accessed July 12, 2016, http://www.newadvent.org/cathen/07674d.htm.

[102] Saint Alphonsus de Liguori, *Glories*, 625.

CHAPTER 13
The Immaculate Heart, the Immaculate Conception, and the Defeat of the Revolution

There Is No Historical Determinism

Divine Providence directs history according to Its plans. Though these plans may not always be understandable to us on this earth, Providence never forces man's free will. Consequently, there is no historical determinism by which all events are completely determined by previously existing causes that exclude man's free will. Nor is there a determinism that would decree that the Revolution must march inevitably forward following its centuries-long process of deterioration of Christendom.

Medieval Christendom consisted of a moral union of European countries under the aegis of the Catholic faith. The Pope was considered the common Father and arbitrator of all peoples. The Renaissance, and later Protestantism, triggered a disintegration of that magnificent order and started a process of decadence that affects all nations.

In spite of this, the Holy Catholic Church never ceases to shine in her saints and her true followers have had numerous victories against the Revolution.

Divine "Slowness" and Human Anxiety

"For a thousand years in thy sight are as yesterday, which is past" (Ps. 89:4).

Sometimes the action of God in history seems too slow to us. More than four thousand years went by between God's promise of the Savior to Adam and Eve and His birth in Bethlehem. So it is not surprising that the promise made at Fatima regarding the triumph of the Immaculate Heart of Mary is a hundred years old and still has not been fulfilled.

On the other hand, from a historical perspective, we oftentimes have difficulty distinguishing the progress of good as it is seemingly intertwined with the spread of evil. In the parable of the wheat and the tares, Our Lord explained that only at the end of time will evil be eradicated from the earth and the wicked sent to eternal fire (cf. Matt. 13: 24-30).

Although the revolutionary process seems to have reached the height of its power in our day—challenging the natural law itself with procured abortion, same-sex "marriage," transgender tyranny, and euthanasia—the Light that shone in the darkness (John 1:5) continues to work in souls and to gain ground, albeit imperceptibly.

Immaculate Conception and Revolutionary Process

There are, however, moments when this Light shines bright for all to see. One of these occasions was the proclamation of the dogma of the Immaculate Conception. This event had a profound impact on the Revolution.

In an article on the centennial of the Lourdes apparitions (February, 1958), after talking about the proclamation of the dogma of the Immaculate Conception by Pius IX in 1854 (confirmed in 1858 by the apparitions of Our Lady in Lourdes), Plinio Corrêa de Oliveira writes:

> The new dogma also deeply shocked the essentially egalitarian mentality of the French Revolution, which since 1789 had despotically held sway in the West. To see a mere creature elevated so far above all others, enjoying an inestimable privilege from the very first instance of her conception is something that could not and cannot fail to hurt the children of a Revolution which proclaimed absolute equality among men as the basis of all order, justice and goodness. It was painful for both non-Catholics and Catholics, more or less infected with this spirit, to accept the fact that God established in creation and highlighted such outstanding inequality.

Further on:

> It is impossible to think about the Immaculate Virgin Mary without recalling how she triumphantly and definitively crushed the serpent's head under her heel. The Revolutionary mentality is

the mentality of the devil himself. A person of faith cannot fail to recognize the role the devil has played in the rise and propagation of the errors of the Revolution, from the religious disasters of the sixteenth century to the political debacle of the eighteenth century and all that followed.

From 1854 onward, the Revolution began to suffer great defeats. There is no doubt the Revolution continued to extend its empire over the earth. Egalitarianism, sensuality, and skepticism attained ever more radical and widespread victories. However, something new appeared. And this something, while seemingly insignificant and self-effacing, is growing irresistibly and will end up killing the Revolution.

The author concludes:

[At] Fatima, Our Lady made it very clear: Either we convert, or a tremendous chastisement will come. However, the Reign of her Immaculate Heart will finally be established in the world. In other words, the Heart of Mary will triumph, be it with more, be it with less human suffering. This means that, according to the message of Fatima, the days of impiety are numbered. The definition of the dogma of the Immaculate Conception marked the beginning of a succession of events that will lead to the Reign of Mary.[103]

Immaculate Conception and Immaculate Heart

The proclamation of the dogma of the Immaculate Conception was essential for the devotion to the Heart of Mary to assume its essential characteristic of *Immaculate.*

Our considerations on the importance of the dogma of the Immaculate Conception for the defeat of the Revolution fully apply, therefore, to the Immaculate Heart of Mary, especially in light of Fatima's promise of ultimate victory: "In the end, my Immaculate Heart will triumph."

---

[103] Plinio Corrêa de Oliveira, "A First Milestone in the Rise of the Counter-Revolution," *Catolicismo*, No. 86, Feb. 1958, accessed July 12, 2016, http://www.tfp.org/tfp-home/about-our-lady/a-first-milestone-in-the-rise-of-the-counter-revolution.html.

CONCLUSION

The Reign of the Immaculate Heart of Mary

At Fatima, Our Lady spoke of a punishment that would come if the world did not convert, and that even "various nations [would] be annihilated." We are currently witnessing that chastisement. The world is plunging deeper into chaos and anarchy. Sadly, we see moral and doctrinal confusion even in the Church.

The Foreseen Chastisement: Punishment and Mercy

This chastisement has two aspects: firstly, the punishment for sins that offend God and require reparation to His justice; and secondly, mercy, so that through suffering, people open up to God's grace, become detached from sin, and turn back to Him again.

This is what explains Professor Corrêa de Oliveira's lifelong dedication to spreading the Fatima message far and wide. During one of his lectures in the early 1970s he commented:

> Great sins bring great punishments on peoples. Great punishments bring great amendments, and great amendments bring great reconciliations. That is in the order of the economy of grace.

After alluding to various historical examples in light of the Fatima message, he concludes:

> If this is not to be the end of the world, then there must be a reconciliation with God as great as the punishment [will be].[104]

In Fatima, Our Lady made it clear that this is not the end of the world when she promised:

> **In the end, my Immaculate Heart will triumph.** The Holy Father will consecrate Russia to me, and she will be converted, and a certain period of peace will be granted to the world.

The "Latter Times"

According to Our Lady's words, there will still be a period of time before the end of the world. As part of the triumph of the

---

[104] Plinio Corrêa de Oliveira, Lecture, Aug. 6, 1971.

Immaculate Heart of Mary it will be a time of glory for Our Lady. Saint Louis-Marie Grignion de Montfort referred to our modern era as the "latter times."

According to this great Marian saint, the "latter times" will precede the final decadence, the Antichrist and the end of the world, and the second coming of Our Lord Jesus Christ to judge the living and the dead. This latter times or great reconciliation mentioned by Professor Corrêa de Oliveira, according to Saint Louis de Montfort, will inaugurate an era of Mary, all imbued with the spirit of the Universal Mediatrix of all Graces:

> Mary must shine forth more than ever in mercy, in might, and in grace, in these latter times: in mercy, to bring back and lovingly receive the poor strayed sinners who shall be converted and shall return to the Catholic Church; in might, against the enemies of God, idolaters, schismatics, Mahometans, Jews, and souls hardened in impiety, who shall rise in terrible revolt against God to seduce all those who shall be contrary to them, and to make them fall by promises and threats; and, finally, she must shine forth in grace, in order to animate and sustain the valiant soldiers and faithful servants of Jesus Christ, who shall do battle for His interests.[105]

The Queenship of Mary

On May 13, 1946, a statue of Our Lady of Fatima was crowned by Benedetto Aloisi Cardinal Masella on behalf of Pope Pius XII. On that occasion, in a radio message to Portugal, the Pontiff thus exalted the Queenship of Mary:

> Our mind... call to acclamations even more ardent, [than those being expressed at Fatima] other triumphs much more divine, another hour—eternally solemn—in the never-ending day of eternity, when the glorious Virgin, entering triumphantly into heaven, was elevated above the hierarchies of the blessed and the angelic choirs to the throne of the most Holy Trinity who, placing on her brow a triple diadem of glory, presented her to

---

[105] de Montfort, *True Devotion*, 19.

the heavenly court seated at the right hand of the immortal King
of the ages and crowned *Queen of the Universe.* [106]

The "Reign of Mary"

As mentioned, after the punishment and conversion—both according to the Fatima message and Saint Louis de Montfort—
there will be a triumph of Our Lady, the "Reign of Mary." This is
simply the Reign of Our Lord Jesus Christ through His Mother:

> It is by the most holy Virgin Mary that Jesus has come into the
> world, and **it is also by her that He has to reign in the world....**
>
> If, then, as is certain, the **kingdom of Jesus Christ is to come
> into the world, it will be but a necessary consequence of the
> knowledge of the kingdom of the most holy Virgin Mary** who
> brought Him into the world the first time, and will make His sec-
> ond advent full of splendor....
>
> When that time comes, wonderful things will happen in those
> lowly places, where the Holy Ghost, finding his dear Spouse as it
> were reproduced in souls, shall come in with abundance, and fill
> them full to overflowing with His gifts, and particularly with the
> gift of wisdom, to work the miracles of grace. My dear brother,
> when will that happy time, that **age of Mary**, come, when souls,
> losing themselves in the abyss of her interior, shall become living
> copies of Mary, to love and glorify Jesus? That time will not come
> until men shall know and practice this devotion which I am teach-
> ing. **Ut adveniat regnum tuum, adveniat regnum Mariae.** [Lord,
> that your kingdom may come, may the reign of Mary come!] [107]

The devotion the saint taught is to consecrate oneself to
Mary Most Holy as a slave of love, giving her everything one is
and has, including one's acquired merits—past, present and fu-
ture—that she may dispose of them as she wishes. Moreover,
the slave of Mary should give his will to her so that he does

---

[106] Pius XII, "Radio Message on the Occasion of the Coronation of the Statue of Our Lady of
Fatima" (May 13, 1946) in *Papal Teachings—Our Lady*, eds. Monks of Solesmes (Boston: Saint
Paul Editions, 1961), 267.

[107] de Montfort, *True Devotion*, 1, 4, 97-8.

nothing in dissonance with Her sovereign will and works for her glory in everything he does.

Triumph of the Immaculate Heart of Mary

The parallels between Saint Louis de Montfort's predictions and considerations and those of Fatima are remarkable. The Reign of Mary, soon to emerge, will be the triumph of the Immaculate Heart of Mary as promised at Fatima.

Prof. Plinio Corrêa de Oliveira explains:

> Specifically, from the Fatima standpoint, the **Reign of Mary** will be the **Reign of the Immaculate Heart of Mary.** That is, a reign of purity and goodness of Our Lady's maternal heart; a reign of great splendor both in temporal society and in the Church, through abundant graces poured out by the Holy Ghost. Indeed, it has always been Church doctrine that the foundation of all excellence in the temporal order is an intimate and faithful union of souls with Our Lord Jesus Christ, Our Lady, His Mother, and the Holy Church, His Mystical Spouse.
>
> From this union derives a faithful observance of the Commandments. And from the latter derives, in turn, an entire and splendorous harmony in human relationships.
>
> So when men practice love of neighbor for the love of God, this gives rise to a vibrant vitality and to a good ordering of all societies, groups, and institutions that make up the temporal sphere, from its basic unit, the family, to the State at its summit.
>
> In turn, as a fruit borne on a tree, all this gives rise to progress of every kind, not only in the temporal sphere but the spiritual one as well.
>
> Peace! There is so much talk about it these days, and yet few know what it is. Even fewer are those who possess it; for true peace is the peace of Christ in the Kingdom of Christ.[108]

---

[108] Plinio Corrêa de Oliveira, *Warriors of the Virgin: The Reply of Authenticity—TFP without Secrets*, accessed Feb. 18, 2016, http://www.pliniocorreadeoliveira.info/GVRA_0009cap9.htm#_ftn2.(Our translation.)

The Queen of Hearts

The Reign of Mary will begin in people's hearts and spread to society as Saint Louis de Montfort explains:

> **Mary is the Queen of heaven and earth by grace, as Jesus is the king of them by nature and by conquest.**
>
> Now, as the kingdom of Jesus Christ consists principally in the heart and interior of a man—according to that word, "The kingdom of God is within you"—in like manner the kingdom of our Blessed Lady is principally in the interior of a man, that is to say, his soul; and it is principally in souls that she is more glorified with her Son than in all visible creatures, and that we can call her, as the Saints do, the Queen of hearts.[109]

In this time of special graces in which Our Lord Jesus will reign through Mary in hearts, souls, and society, the Mother of God will communicate her spirit to many. The faith and charity of the saints, the courage of the martyrs, and the strength and combativeness of the crusaders will once again shine on earth.

When Pope Pius XII established the feast of Mary the Queen, he showed how maternal her queenship is and urged everyone to approach her throne with confidence:

> Let all, therefore, try to approach with greater trust the throne of grace and mercy of **our Queen and Mother**, and beg for strength in adversity, light in darkness, consolation in sorrow; above all let them strive to free themselves from the slavery of sin and offer an unceasing homage, **filled with filial loyalty, to their Queenly Mother.** Let her churches be thronged by the faithful, her feast-days honored; **may the beads of the Rosary be in the hands of all**; may Christians gather, in small numbers and large, to sing her praises in churches, in homes, in hospitals, in prisons. May Mary's name be held in highest reverence, a name sweeter than honey and more precious than jewels; may none utter blasphemous words, the sign of a defiled soul, against that name graced with such dignity and revered for its motherly goodness; let no one be so bold as to speak a syllable which lacks the respect due to her name.[110]

---

[109] *True Devotion*, 14.

[110] Pius XII, Encyclical *Ad Caeli Reginam* (On Proclaiming the Queenship of Mary), Oct. 11, 1954, accessed Mar. 15, 2016, http://w2.vatican.va/content/pius-xii/en/encyclicals/documents/hf_p-xii_enc_11101954_ad-caeli-reginam.html.

On another occasion, the same Pope presented the Reign of Mary as the solution for today's problems:

> While the world at present struggles unceasingly to achieve unity and insure peace, **the invocation of Mary's reign**—surpassing all earthly means and all human plans, which are always in some way defective—is the voice of Christian faith and hope, strengthened and reinforced by divine promises and by the inexhaustible aid which Mary's rule has provided for the salvation of mankind.[111]

Ardent Supplication for the Reign of Mary

However much the horizon is now obscured, confidence in the promise made by Our Lady at Fatima that her Immaculate Heart will triumph is the reason we can be calm during the looming storm.

Above all, we must seize the opportunity of this centennial of the apparitions of Our Lady at Fatima to increase our fervor. Let us beseech Heaven that Mary Most Holy hasten the triumph of her Immaculate Heart and the coming of the Reign of Mary!

The Reign of Mary, Plinio Corrêa de Oliveira said, will not only be a victory of Our Lady but a glorious triumph:

> [In Fatima] Our Lady did not say "My Immaculate Heart will win," but used an expression with sharply different hues. There is a difference between a victory and a triumph. A triumph is not just any win. It is a great victory, a remarkable victory! Our Lady announces her triumph, that is, a glorious victory in which she will completely master the situation. We will have the Reign of Mary, therefore, for one cannot understand that she would win without becoming Queen.[112]

---

[111] Pius XII, "Allocution in Saint Peter Basilica," Nov. 1, 1954, in *Solesmes, Papal Teachings–Our Lady*, 411.

[112] Plinio Corrêa de Oliveira, Lecture, July 14, 1971.

APPENDIX I

"Russia Will Already Have Scattered her Errors Throughout the World"
(Reprinted from Chapter 14 of *Fatima: A Message More Urgent than Ever*)

The request for the consecration of Russia to the Immaculate Heart of Mary was made on June 13, 1929, the twelfth anniversary of the second apparition. As Sister Lúcia recounts, she was making a vigil of prayers alone in the chapel between 11 p.m. and midnight, when she had a symbolic vision about the Most Blessed Trinity and the Redemption.

The Solemnity of the Request

Suddenly, the whole chapel was illuminated with a supernatural light and on the altar appeared a cross that went all the way to the ceiling. In a brighter light one saw, on the upper part of the cross, the face of a man and his torso down to his waist, on his chest a dove and, nailed to the cross, the body of another man. A little below the waist [of the crucified], suspended in the air, one saw a Chalice and a large Host upon which were falling some drops of blood that ran down the face of the crucified and from a wound in his chest. Running down the Host, those drops fell inside the Chalice. Under the right arm of the cross was Our Lady with her Immaculate Heart in her hand (it was Our Lady of Fatima with her Immaculate Heart in her left hand, without sword or roses but with a crown of thorns and flames). Under the left arm [of the cross] large letters resembling crystalline waters running down on top of the altar, formed the words "Grace and Mercy."

The seer understood that it was an allusion to the mystery of the Most Holy Trinity, about which, she says, she received insights that she was not allowed to communicate.

In that context full of mystery and grandeur, the Mother of God addressed her, saying, "The moment has arrived wherein God is asking the Holy Father, in union with all the bishops of the world, to consecrate Russia to my Immaculate Heart. He promises to save [Russia] by this means."

The Advance of Socialism

The request could not have been made in a more solemn and imperative fashion. Nor could the moment be more opportune. In 1929, communism had already consolidated its power in Russia and spread to the whole world through parties directed by Moscow. Russia (or communism) was "spreading its errors throughout the world."

In Mexico, the Church was being persecuted by revolutionary socialist governments; in France, the radical government prepared to sign the Franco-Soviet accord of mutual assistance; in Spain, a socialist republic was about to be installed with churches being set on fire, persecutions and slaughter of Catholics and the clergy, and a bloody Civil War.

Although Nazism and the Fascist movements that appeared at that time were presented as political enemies of communism, their ideological underpinning was also socialist—State preeminence over the individual, total control over education and the economy, the worship of force, and the amoral tenet that the end justifies the means. Above all, Nazism and Fascism shared pagan materialism and naturalism, which denies the supernatural order and transforms man into a "superman" or "demiurge."

Pope Pius XI Receives the Request for the Consecration

Sister Lúcia, as she herself confirmed, passed Our Lady's request on to her confessor, who in turn forwarded it to Pope Pius XI. Indeed, in a letter written to Pope Pius XII in 1940, she says about that communication:

> In 1929, Our Lady, in another apparition, asked for the consecration of Russia to Her Immaculate Heart, promising by that means to prevent the propagation of its errors, and its conversion.

Some time later, I informed my confessor of Our Lady's request. His Reverence employed some means to have it forwarded to His Holiness Pius XI.

Likewise, on February 3, 1946, during an interview with Father Hubert Jongen, a young Dutch Montfortian priest, he asked if Pius XI had known about the request. Sister Lúcia answered, "Father José Bernardo Gonçalves [my confessor] . . . informed His Grace the Bishop of Leiria about everything, and managed for the request to come to the knowledge of H.H. Pius XI."

The next year, she gave an almost identical response to Father Thomas McGlynn, O.P., an American priest. He asked, "Was this wish made known to the Holy Father at that time?" Sister Lúcia replied, "I told my confessor; he informed the Bishop of Leiria. After a while my confessor said that the communication had been sent to the Holy Father."

The Consecration Was Not Made at the Proper Time
We do not have elements to know the reasons why Pope Pius XI did not make the requested consecration, all the more so since he believed in the authenticity of the apparitions and was a devotee of Our Lady of Fatima. Already in 1929 the Holy Father had given an unofficial approval to the apparitions by distributing holy cards of Our Lady of Fatima to the seminarians of the Portuguese College of Rome. That was before the official recognition by the Bishop of Leiria, which was done in a pastoral letter in 1930.

What is certain is that Pope Pius XI, who reigned from 1922 to 1939, was supposed to make the requested consecration. This can be understood from the very words of Our Lady at the July 13th apparition, enunciating the reasons why she would come and ask for the consecration, as well as the spreading of the Communion of Reparation on the five First Saturdays. It seems the case to repeat them here:

You have seen Hell, where the souls of poor sinners go. To save them, God wishes to establish devotion to my Immaculate Heart in the world. If they do what I will tell you, many souls will be saved, and there will be peace. The war is going to end. But if they do not stop offending God, another even worse war will begin in the reign of Pius XI. When you see a night illuminated by an unknown light, know that it is the great sign that God gives you that He is going to punish the world for its crimes by means of war, hunger, and persecutions against the Church and the Holy Father.

To prevent it, I will come to ask for the consecration of Russia to my Immaculate Heart and the Communion of Reparation on the First Saturdays. If they listen to my requests, Russia will be converted and there will be peace. If not, she will scatter her errors throughout the world, provoking wars and persecutions of the Church. The good will be martyred, the Holy Father will have much to suffer and various nations will be annihilated. In the end, My Immaculate Heart will triumph. The Holy Father will consecrate Russia to me and she will be converted and a certain period of peace will be granted to the world.

So we see that Our Lady indicated a general means for the salvation of souls, which is devotion to her Immaculate Heart: "To save them, God wishes to establish devotion to my Immaculate Heart in the world."

Then she indicated, within this general means, that is, devotion to the Immaculate Heart of Mary, some specific means to obtain certain ends, namely the conversion of Russia, to avoid the war and all its consequences, including the dissemination of the "errors of Russia," persecutions of the Church and the Holy Father, the martyrdom of the good, the annihilation of many nations.

The specific means indicated were the consecration of Russia to the Immaculate Heart of Mary and the Communion of Reparation of the five First Saturdays. Indeed, soon after speaking about the new war that would break out at the time of Pope Pius XI if her requests were not heeded, i.e., the Second World War, and the dissemination of the errors of Russia, and so forth, the Most Holy Virgin says, "To prevent it, I will come to ask for the consecration of Russia to My Immaculate Heart and the

Communion of Reparation on the First Saturdays."

It is quite obvious that in the phrase, "to prevent it,"[113] the pronoun "it" refers to what had been mentioned earlier: the war and all its consequences that would ensue if the request were not heeded.

Therefore, it is entirely clear that the consecration of Russia to the Immaculate Heart of Mary was the means to avoid the Second World War and the brutal spread of communism that followed it. So the consecration had to be done before the world conflict broke out; for if one must do *A* to prevent *B* from happening, one must do *A* before *B* happens.

Thus, for the consecration of Russia to have the effect desired by the Blessed Mother, it should have been made in the time span between 1929, the date it was requested, and 1939, the beginning of the Second World War. Now then, that period coincides with Pope Pius XI's pontificate, who was elected on February 6, 1922 and died on February 10, 1939.

The Consecration Should Have Been Made as Soon as It Was Asked

Now then, as we have seen above, in 1938 there was already a state of war. In fact, many historians consider the *Anschluss*, the annexation of Austria and its occupation by German troops on March 12, 1938, as part of World War II. Likewise, in the Munich Accord of September 1938, Germany obtained from France and Great Britain their *placet* to the annexation of the Sudetenland.

So, it would seem that in order to obtain the desired effects, the consecration of Russia to the Immaculate Heart of Mary should have been made before 1938. More likely, however, it should have been made in the beginning of the 1930s to avoid the great Communist advance that took place in that decade,

---

[113] In the original: "[N]o reinado de Pio XI começará outra guerra..... Para a impedir, virei pedir a consagração da Russia...." Now then, in Portuguese the demonstrative pronoun "a" is feminine and singular, and therefore it is replacing a feminine singular noun, that is, "guerra" war.

the tragedy in Spain, as well as to stop Nazi Germany's quest for expansion that would lead to worldwide conflagration.

Everything indicates, therefore, that the appropriate time for the consecration was precisely the moment when it was requested: around 1929–1930, perhaps even in 1935, before the Spanish Civil War. In any case, that consecration could never be done after World War II had begun, at least as a condition to avoid it, as had been promised at Fatima.

A Documented Confirmation

In many supernatural manifestations to Sister Lúcia, Our Lord and Our Lady complained that the consecration had not been done and said that when it was done it would already be too late. In a letter of January 21, 1935, Sister Lúcia writes Father Gonçalves, "As for Russia, it seems to me that Our Lord will be very pleased with your work for the Holy Father to fulfill His desires. Some three years ago Our Lord was very unhappy because His request was not fulfilled. . . . "

In another letter to the same priest, on May 18, 1936:

> As for the other question: If it would be well to insist in order to obtain the consecration of Russia. I answer almost the same as I have the other times. I am sorry it has not yet been done . . . I have spoken intimately with Our Lord about the matter, and just recently I asked Him why would He not convert Russia without His Holiness having made this consecration. [He answered], "Because I want My whole Church to acknowledge that consecration as a triumph of the Immaculate Heart of Mary, so that it may extend devotion to it and place devotion to this Immaculate Heart beside the devotion to My Sacred Heart."

Sister Lúcia insists that the pope would not believe her words if God himself did not change his heart. To which Our Lord answers, "The Holy Father! Pray very much for the Holy Father. He will do it, but it will be too late! Nevertheless, the Immaculate Heart of Mary will save Russia. It has been entrusted to Her."

Our Lady refers to the conversion of Russia after the triumph of the Immaculate Heart of Mary, that is, after the trials of the chastisement, as stated in the message of July, 1917:

> "[Russia] will scatter her errors throughout the world, provoking wars and persecutions of the Church. The good will be martyred, the Holy Father will have much to suffer and various nations will be annihilated. In the end, my Immaculate Heart will triumph. The Holy Father will consecrate Russia to me and she will be converted and a certain period of peace will be granted to the world."

On another occasion, Our Lord communicated to Sister Lúcia:

> "They did not want to fulfill my request. Like the king of France, **they will repent and will do it but it will be too late. Russia will already have scattered her errors throughout the world, provoking wars and persecutions of the Church:** The Holy Father will have much to suffer."[114]

In October, 1940, when Sister Lúcia wrote to Pope Pius XII proposing that the consecration of the world be made with a special mention of Russia, she no longer says that the consecration can avoid the chastisement but only that it can "abbreviate the days of tribulation with which [God] has determined to punish the nations for their crimes through war, hunger and many persecutions of the Church and of Your Holiness."

The Consecrations

Undoubtedly, the chastisement predicted in case Russia was not consecrated to the Immaculate Heart of Mary has not ended. The consecrations carried out afterwards were

---

[114] This is an allusion to the promise Our Lord made to Louis XIV through Saint Margaret Mary Alacoque. Our Lord promised to grant the king a life of grace and eternal glory, as well as victory over his enemies, if he would consecrate himself to the Sacred Heart, let it reign in his palace, paint it on his banners, and have it engraved on his coat of arms. As of 1792, after Louis XVI had been imprisoned in the Tower of the Temple, this request had still not been heeded. This king then made the vow to consecrate himself, his family, and his kingdom to the Sacred Heart of Jesus if he regained his freedom, the crown, and royal power. It was too late: the king left prison only for his execution.

certainly pleasing to God but, as the historical events clearly show, they no longer had the power to forestall the chastisement.

Here are the consecrations:

Pope Pius XII: On October 31, 1942, consecrated the Church and the human race to the Immaculate Heart of Mary, and on July 7, 1952, he consecrated the Russians to the Immaculate Heart of Mary.

Pope Paul VI: On November 21, 1964, confided the human race to the Immaculate Heart of Mary.

Pope John Paul II made two consecrations of the world to the Immaculate Heart of Mary: in Fatima on May 13, 1982; and in Rome on March 25, 1984.

Pope Benedict XVI on May 13, 2007 invoking Our Lady of Fatima on the ninetieth anniversary of the apparitions, stated, "In a special way we entrust to Mary those peoples and nations that are in particular need, confident that she will not fail to heed the prayers we make to her with filial devotion."

APPENDIX II

The Immaculate Heart of Mary and the Chastisement Foretold at Fatima

For all that we have seen about the motherly kindness of the Immaculate Heart of Mary, many of you may wonder how that kindness is consistent with the announcement of a punishment for humanity.

We have already explained elsewhere the twofold purpose of divine punishment on this earth: to make reparation for God's offended justice and to bring sinners to repentance and conversion (this is the "remedial" aspect of punishment).

Love of Divine Justice
But there is another point to consider: the relationship between the Immaculate Heart and the first aspect of punishment, that is, making reparation to Divine justice.

Since the love of God in the Blessed Mother is most perfect, it cannot be limited to divine mercy but must also extend to God's justice, as both are attributes of God. And since in God everything is perfect, Divine justice is as worthy of adoration as all His other attributes.

Moreover, as Saint Thomas Aquinas teaches, Divine justice and mercy are so linked together that one does not exist without the other. Mercy is active even when justice punishes an unrepentant sinner with the pains of hell. Indeed, while not preventing the execution of the sentence, mercy makes the reprobate suffer less than he deserves. [115]

The sublime love of the Immaculate Heart of Mary for God's mercy and justice makes us understand why she herself

---

[115] "Even in the damnation of the reprobate mercy is seen, which, though it does not totally remit, yet somewhat alleviates, in punishing short of what is deserved." (*Summa Theologica*, q. 21 a. 4 ad 1.)

maternally came to warn of the divine punishment if men did not stop offending God.

Admirable Explanation of Saint John Eudes

Saint John Eudes (1601-1680), one of the great propagators of devotion to the Immaculate Heart of Mary, admirably explains the love of the Blessed Virgin for Divine justice.

In the third chapter of his masterful book *The Admirable Heart of Mary,* titled *The Justice of God Mirrored in the Admirable Heart of Mary,* he writes:

> "MERCY and justice resemble two sisters, inseparable and holding each other by the hand. Wherever mercy is, there also is justice; where justice goes, mercy follows. Hence King David sang to God: 'Mercy and judgment I will sing to thee, O Lord.'"[116]

He mentions them together and does not separate these qualities. Continuing, he writes:

> "If the Holy Heart of Mary is filled with such terrible hatred of sin that she consented to the cruel death of her beloved Son, because she saw Him loaded with the sins of men; if she readily sacrificed Him to divine justice in order to crush the mortal enemy of God and men, who can doubt that she still hates the infernal monster wherever she finds it? She hates sin to the point of sometimes uniting herself to divine vengeance in order to destroy it in souls, especially in those souls who are their own enemies to the extent of supporting evil and opposing its destruction. They force their sweet Mother, as it were, to relinquish the tenderness of her maternal love and to participate in the severity of divine justice in order to punish the obduracy of a rebellious soul hardened in malice.

> "O most holy Virgin, since thou hast but one Heart and one spirit with thy divine Son and since thou hast no other sentiments save His, thou dost love what He loves and thou dost hate what He hates. Hence, as Christ has an infinite hatred for sin, thou also dost hate it beyond all thought and words. Thy hatred for the infernal monster is equal to the love thou hast for God. O Blessed Mother, the love of thy Heart for God is infinitely greater than that of all the hearts of the angels and saints. Consequently, there is in thy Heart

---

[116] Ps. 100:1.

more hatred against God's enemy, sin, than in the hearts of all heaven's citizens. Make us sharers, O Mary, in this love and hatred so that we may love our Creator and Savior as thou hast loved Him, and that we may hate sin as thou hast hated it."[117]

Saint Alphonsus de Liguori: The Abuse of Mercy Leads to Hell

Given the love of the Immaculate Heart for Divine justice, we understand better not only why she announced a punishment for sinful humanity, but also why she showed hell to the three shepherd children, explaining, "You have seen hell, where the souls of poor sinners go." And she maternally added: "In order to save them, God wants to establish devotion to my Immaculate Heart in the world."

In fact, there is much talk about mercy but little is said about the justice of God, causing many to get a notion of mercy as being separate from Divine justice. With that, people indulge in a life of sin or at least one of unconcern about eternal salvation. Therefore, as we explain Our Lady's love both for God's mercy and His justice, it is very timely to reproduce here the fiery words of the great Saint Alphonsus de Liguori in one of his sermons:

> "'**But God is merciful.**' Behold another common delusion by which the devil encourages sinners to persevere in a life of sin! A certain author has said that more souls have been sent to hell by the mercy of God than by His justice. This is indeed the case; for men are induced by the deceits of the devil to persevere in sin, through confidence in God's mercy; and thus they are lost.

> "God is merciful. Who denies it? But, great as His mercy is, how many does He every day send to hell? God is merciful, but He is also just, and is, therefore, obliged to punish those who offend him. And 'His mercy,' says the divine mother, extends 'to them that fear him.' (Luke 1:50.) But with regard to those who abuse His mercy and despise Him, He exercises justice.

---

[117] Saint John Eudes, *The Admirable Heart of Mary* (New York: P. J. Kenedy & Sons, 1948), 144-6.

"The Lord pardons sins, but he cannot pardon the determination to commit sin. Saint Augustine says, that he who sins with the intention of repenting after his sins, is not a penitent but a scoffer. *Irrisor est non poenitens.* But the Apostle tells us that God will not be mocked. 'Be not deceived; God is not mocked.' (Gal. 6:7) It would be a mockery of God to insult Him as often and as much as you pleased, and afterwards to expect eternal glory."[118]

---

[118] Saint Alphonsus de Liguori, *Sermons For All the Sundays in the Year*, eighth edition (James Duffy & Sons, 15 Wellington Quay; 1882) 109.

Bibliography

Alonso, CMF, Joaquin Maria. "La Consagración al Corazón de Maria—Una Síntesis Teológica." In José Maria Canal, CMF, *La Consagración al Corazón de María.* Madrid: Editorial Coculsa, 1960.

Aquinas, Saint Thomas. *Summa Theologica.* Accessed July 12, 2016. http://www.newadvent.org/summa/3082.htm.

Sententia libri Ethicorum. Accessed July 12, 2016. http://www.corpusthomisticum.org/ctc08.html.

The Catena Aurea Gospel of Saint Luke. Accessed July 12, 2016. http://dhspriory.org/thomas/english/CALuke.htm.

Brien, SJ, L. "La dévotion au Cœur Immaculé de Marie." In *Par Marie à la Céleste Patrie,* Synthèse de la Théologie, Vol. VIII. Montréal: Éditions de l'Institut Pie-XI, 1956, 127-8.

Canal, CMF, José Maria. *La Consagración a la Virgen y a su Corazón.* Madrid: Editorial Coculsa, 1960.

Center for Applied Research in the Apostolate. *Frequently Requested Church Statistics.* Accessed Mar. 14, 2016. http://cara.georgetown.edu/frequently-requested-church-statistics/

Corrêa de Oliveira, Plinio. "A First Milestone in the Rise of the Counter-Revolution." *Catolicismo*, No. 86, Feb. 1958. Accessed July 12, 2016. http://www.tfp.org/tfp-home/about-our-lady/a-first-milestone-in-the-rise-of-the-counter-revolution.html.

"Books v. Cannons." *Legionário,* Apr. 8, 1945. Accessed Mar. 14, 2016. http://www.pliniocorreadeoliveira.info/LEG%2045-04-08_Livrosversuscanhoes.htm.

"Consecration to Our Lady." *Legionário*, No. 675, July 15, 1945.

"Dead? Or Red? The Great Crossroads of Our Times from the Standpoint of the Fatima Message." *Catolicismo*, No. 411, Mar. 1985.

"Hodie in Terra Canunt Angeli, Laetantur Archangeli, Hodie exultant Justi – The Voice of Fatima." *Catolicismo*, No. 84, Dec. 1957.

"Holy Intransigence, an Aspect of the Immaculate Conception." *Catolicismo*, No. 45, Sept. 1954.

Lecture, July 14, 1971. (Archives of the Plinio Corrêa de Oliveira Commission).

Lecture, Nov. 25, 1974.

Lecture, Aug. 6, 1971.

"Pius XII and the Era of Mary." *Catolicismo*, No. 48, Dec. 1954.

Revolution and Counter-Revolution. York, Penn.: The American Society for the Defense of Tradition, Family, and Property, 1993. Accessed July 12, 2016. http://www.tfp.org/tfp-home/books/revolution-and-counter-revolution-v15-1370.html.

"The Consecration to the Immaculate Heart of Mary." *Ave Maria* (São Paulo), No. 31, July 1943. Accessed Feb. 27, 2016. http://www.pliniocorreadeoliveira.info/OUT%20-%20194307_A%20Consagra%C3%A7%C3%A3o%20ao%20Imaculado%20Cora%C3%A7%C3%A3o%20de%20Maria.htm.

"The Queenship of Our Lady and the Wise and Immaculate Heart of Mary," Lecture, May 31, 1975. Accessed Feb. 26, 2016. http://www.pliniocorreadeoliveira.info/DIS_SD_750531_Sapiencial_Coracao_de_Maria.htm#.VtC4vNAwCZM.

Warriors of the Virgin: The Reply of Authenticity—TFP without Secrets. Accessed Feb. 18, 2016. http://www.pliniocorreadeoliveira.info/GVRA_0009cap9.htm#_ftn2.

Courtois, Stephane and Nicholas Werth, Jean-Louis Panné, Andrzej Paczkowski, Karel Bartošek, and Jean-Louis Margolin. *The Black Book of Communism: Crimes, Terror, Repression*. Edited by

Mark Kramer. Translated by Jonathan Murphy. Cambridge, Mass.: Harvard University Press, 1999.

de Finance, SJ, Joseph. "Consécration." In *Dictionnaire de Spiritualité*, vol. II, cols. 1575-1583.

de Liguori, Saint Alphonsus. *The Glories of Mary*. New York: P.J. Kenedy & Sons, 1888.

Sermons For All the Sundays In The Year, eighth edition. Dublin: James Duffy & Sons, 15 Wellington Quay; 1882.

de Montfort, Saint Louis. *True Devotion To Mary*. Spring Grove, Penn.: The American Society for the Defense of Tradition, Family, and Property, 2013.

Ephrem the Syrian, Saint. *Precationes ad Deiparam*. In *Opp. Graec. Lat.*, Vol. III, 524-37. In Holweck, F. "Immaculate Conception." In *The Catholic Encyclopedia*. New York: Robert Appleton Company, 1910. Accessed July 12, 2016. http://www.newadvent.org/cathen/07674d.htm.

Guldner, Benedict. "Conversion." In *The Catholic Encyclopedia*, Vol. IV. New York: Robert Appleton Company, 1908.

Horvat II, John. *Return to Order: From a Frenzied Economy to an Organic Christian Society—Where We've Been, How We Got Here, and Where We Need to Go*. York, Penn.: York Press, 2013.

Léon-Dufour, Xavier. *Vocabulário de Teologia Bíblica*. Petrópolis: Vozes, 1992.

Leo XIII. Encyclical *Annum Sacrum*. Accessed July 12, 2016. http://w2.vatican.va/content/leo-xiii/en/encyclicals/documents/hf_l-xiii_enc_25051899_annum-sacrum.html.

Marin, SJ, Hilario. *El Corazón de Maria en el Magisterio de la Iglesia*. Madrid: Editorial Coculsa, 1960.

Mossman, Thomas W., trans. *The Great Commentary of Cornelius à Lapide, The Holy Gospel according Saint Mark [and] Saint Luke.* Reviewed and completed by Michael J. Miller. Fitzwilliam, N.H.: Loreto Publications, 2008.

Peinador, CMF, Maximo. *Teologia Biblica Cordimariana.* Madrid: Editorial Coculsa, 1959.

Pius IX. Apostolic Constitution *Ineffabilis Deus.* Accessed May 18, 2016. http://www.papalencyclicals.net/Pius09/p9ineff.htm.

Pius XI. Encyclical *Miserentissimus Redemptor.* Accessed May 20, 2016. http://w2.vatican.va/content/pius-xi/en/encyclicals/documents/hf_p-xi_enc_19280508_miserentissimus-redemptor.html.

Pius XII. "Allocution in Saint Peter Basilica," Nov. 1, 1954. In *Papal Teachings—Our Lady*, edited by the Monks of Solesmes. Boston: Saint Paul Editions, 1961, 411.

Encyclical *Ad Caeli Reginam.* Accessed Mar. 15, 2016. http://w2.vatican.va/content/pius-xii/en/encyclicals/documents/hf_p-xii_enc_11101954_ad-caeli-reginam.html.

Encyclical *Haurietis Aquas.* Accessed Mar. 14, 2016. http://www.vatican.va/holy_father/pius_xii/encyclicals/documents/hf_p-xii_enc_15051956_haurietis-aquas_en.html.

"Radio Message on the Occasion of the Coronation of the Statue of Our Lady of Fatima" (May 13, 1946). In *Papal Teachings—Our Lady*, edited by the Monks of Solesmes. Boston: Saint Paul Editions, 1961.

Radio Message to the National Marian Congress in Spain, Oct. 12, 1954. In *Discorsi e Radiomessasaggi*, vol. XVI, 197.

Salverri, SJ, Joaquín. *De la Iglesia de Jesucristo.* Vol. III of *Suma de la Sagrada Teología Escolástica.* Edited by Padres de la Compañía de Jesús. Accessed July 12, 2016. http://www.mercaba.org/TEO-

LOGIA/STE/iglesia/libro_3_cap_2.htm#Articulo%20V.

Schulte, A. J. "Consecration." In *The Catholic Encyclopedia*, Vol. IV. New York: Robert Appleton Company, 1908.

Solimeo, Gustavo Antonio and Luiz Sérgio Solimeo. *Grassroots Church Communities (GRCGs): Perestroika in Latin America?* Carmel, N.Y.: Western Hemisphere Cultural Society, Inc., 1991.

Solimeo, Luiz Sérgio. *Fatima: A Message More Urgent Than Ever.* Spring Grove, Penn.: The American Society for the Defense of Tradition, Family and Property-TFP, 2008.

Teresa of Ávila, Saint. *Las Moradas.* Accessed Jan. 21, 2016. http://hjg.com.ar/teresa_moradas/moradas_6_10.html.

The Seven Dolors of the Blessed Virgin Mary. Accessed Mar. 14, 2016. http://www.ewtn.com/library/MARY/DOLORS.htm.

Wineripdec, Michael. "The Vanishing of the Nuns." *New York Times*, Dec. 2, 2012. Accessed Mar. 14, 2016. http://www.ny-times.com/2012/12/02/booming/the-vanishing-of-the-nuns.html.

Winfield, Nicole and Ines San Martin. "Cardinals Publicly Battling over Divorce." Accessed Mar. 14, 2016. http://www.cruxnow.com/church/2014/09/18/walter-kasper-cardinals-debate-marriage-ahead-of-crucial-meeting/.

Index